Podcast Creation 101

101

Co-Author of Amazon.com
bestseller START HERE

MARSHALL MORRIS

with Former U.S. Small
Business Administration
Entreprenuer of the Year

CLAY CLARK

THE PROVEN PATH TO PODCASTING SUCCESS

*Founders of the
iTunes Top 10
Thrive Time Show
Business Podcast*

D1478875

Podcast Creation 101: The Proven Path to Podcasting Success

ISBN 978-0-692-05128-3

Copyright © 2018 by Marshall Morris and Clay Clark

Thrive Publishing

Published by Thrive Publishing

1100 Suite #100 Riverwalk Terrace

Jenks, OK 74037

Thrive Publishing books may be purchased for educational, business or sales promotional use. For more information, please email the Special Markets Department at info@Thrive15.com. When crossing the street, please look both ways and do not stop, drop, and roll.

TABLE OF CONTENTS

AUTHOR'S NOTE

In every business and every project there must be one chief and one boss because anything with two heads is a monster.

Clay Clark
(Former U.S. Small Business Administration Entrepreneur of the Year)

For this project, Marshall Morris is leading the dance and teaching you about a subject that he knows far better than almost anyone else on the planet. Having had the honor to know and work with Marshall for the past 9 years, I can assure you that Marshall knows what he is talking about. As a business coach I've seen him help countless small business owners to achieve their goals of earning both time freedom and financial freedom and along the way he has helped many entrepreneurs to create podcasts as well. I can assure you that you will not find a more in depth and well-researched "how to podcast book" on the planet and potentially anywhere else in the Universe (I hear the martians and the Illuminati are really into podcasting as well these days) Throughout this book, I will be chiming in with **FUN FACTS, NOTABLE QUOTABLES** and **AMPLE EXAMPLES,** but beyond that you will be reading the thoughts of one of our organization's finest people, Marshall Morris.

FUN FACTS

"Advertisers are expected to spend about $35.1 million (in 2017) on podcasts this year, up about 2% from last year, according to ZenithOptimedia, which is owned by ad holding company Publicis. Meanwhile, marketers are still investing some $18 billion a year in radio and $67 billion in TV."

STEVEN PERLBERG
Podcasts Face Advertising Hurdles
The Wall Street Journal

"About 17% of Americans over the age of 12—around 46 million people—listen to at least one podcast each month, up from just 9% in 2008, according to estimates from Edison Research last year."

STEVEN PERLBERG
Podcasts Face Advertising Hurdles
The Wall Street Journal

INTRODUCTION

"Here's to the crazy ones. The misfits. The rebels. The troublemakers. The round pegs in the square holes. The ones who see things differently. They're not fond of rules. And they have no respect for the status quo. You can quote them, disagree with them, glorify or vilify them. About the only thing you can't do is ignore them. Because they change things. They push the human race forward. And while some may see them as the crazy ones, we see genius. Because the people who are crazy enough to think they can change the world, are the ones who do."

STEVE JOBS
Apple Computer Commercial, 1997

So you've decided that you are crazy enough to want to start a podcast? And you believe that you actually have something to say that other humans will want to listen to? That's pretty bold, my friend. Are you saying that you actually have the audacity to believe other people will listen to and benefit from hearing your voice? Wow. You either have an ego problem or you are just right.

"Whether you think you can, or you think you can't – you're right."

HENRY FORD
(While working as an engineer for the Edison Illuminating Company in Detroit, Henry Ford [1863-1947] built his first gasoline-powered horseless carriage, the Quadricycle, in the shed behind his home)

Here is the thing, we believe in YOU, but YOU have to believe in YOU or this entire podcasting thing is going to be nothing more than a time-wasting experiment for you. Podcasting is a trend that has taken the world by storm over the last 15 years. As an easy-to-consume, niche content vehicle for your ideas, stories, and opinions, podcasting has become one of the most popular ways for an average human (you're above average, though) to create an expert platform. Today you can find podcasts on fantasy football, world politics, and specific niches like historical crime and drug enforcement policies.

FUN FACTS

"The results are in! Thirty-one percent of podcast listeners earn upwards of $100,000 per year and monthly listeners have increased from 21% to 24% according to Edison Research."

OMAID HOMAYUN
9 Podcasts That Will Make You 10% Smarter
Forbes

As you embark into the world of podcasting, you will find that MOST podcasters are NOT SUCCESSFUL because their podcast is NOT GOOD. However, you will also discover that the top podcasters in the world have advertisers lining up to pay them for the opportunity to advertise on their show.

FUN FACTS

According to PodcastChart.com as of September 2017, the following podcasts are the most listened to shows:

1. **The Game of Thrones Podcast**
   They review each week's episode of HBO's Game of Thrones and your feedback to each episode.

2. **Locked Up Abroad**
   What does it feel like in the split second when you realize you're about to be locked up in a foreign country - possibly for life? In Locked Up Abroad, host Jim Clemente (Real Crime Profile) brings you first hand accounts from people who lived this nightmare, starting with Billy Hayes, subject of the Oliver Stone movie Midnight Express. A riveting, immersive audio adaptation of the hit TV series by the National Geographic Channel.

3. **Revisionist History by Malcolm Gladwell**
   Revisionist History is Malcolm Gladwell's journey through the overlooked and the misunderstood. Every episode re-examines something from the past—an event, a person, an idea, even a song—and asks whether we got it right the first time. From Panoply Media. Because sometimes the past deserves a second chance.

4. **Stuff You Should Know**
   How do landfills work? How do mosquitos work? Join Josh and Chuck as they explore the Stuff You Should Know.

5. **TED Radio Hour**
   The TED Radio Hour is a journey through fascinating ideas: astonishing inventions, fresh approaches to old problems, new ways to think and create. Based on talks given by riveting speakers on the world-renowned TED stage, each show is centered on a common theme – such as the source of happiness, crowd-sourcing innovation, power shifts, or inexplicable connections. The TED Radio Hour is hosted by Guy Raz, and is a co-production of NPR & TED. Follow the show @ TEDRadioHour.

6. **S-Town**
   S-Town is a new podcast about a man named John who despises his Alabama town and decides to do something about it. He asks Brian to investigate the son of a wealthy family who's allegedly been bragging that he got away with murder. But when someone else ends up dead, the search for the truth leads to a nasty feud, a hunt for hidden treasure, and an unearthing of the mysteries of one man's life.

7. **The American Life**
   This American Life is a weekly public radio show, heard by 2.2 million people on more than 500 stations. Another 2.5 million people download the weekly podcast. It is hosted by Ira Glass, produced in collaboration with Chicago Public Media, delivered to stations by PRX The Public Radio Exchange, and has won all of the major broadcasting awards.

8. **The Daily**
   This moment demands an explanation. This show is on a mission to find it. Only what you want to know, none of what you don't. Hosted by Michael Barbaro. Powered by New York Times journalism. Twenty minutes a day, five days a week, ready by 6 a.m.

9. **30 for 30 Podcasts**
   Original audio documentaries from the makers of the acclaimed 30 for 30 series. Sports stories like you've never heard before.

10. **A Piece of Work**
    From listener-supported WNYC Studios and MoMA, A Piece of Work is everything you want to know about modern and contemporary art but were afraid to ask. Hosted by Broad City's Abbi Jacobson, this 10-episode series explores everything from Pop Art to performance in lively conversations with curators, artists, and Abbi's friends, including Hannibal Buress, Tavi Gevinson, RuPaul, and Questlove. WNYC Studios is the producer of other leading podcasts including Freakonomics Radio, Death, Sex & Money...

"Be so good they can't ignore you."

STEVE MARTIN
*(Martin's first job was at Disneyland, selling
guidebooks on weekends and full-time during the
school's summer break. This lasted for three years
(1955–1958). During his free time, he frequented
the Main Street Magic shop, where tricks were
demonstrated to potential customers. While working
at Disneyland, he was captured in the background of
the home movie that was made into the short-subject
film Disneyland Dream, coincidentally becoming
his first film appearance. By 1960, he had mastered
several of the tricks and illusions and took a paying
job at the magic shop in Fantasyland in August.
There he perfected his talents for magic, juggling,
and creating balloon animals in the manner of his
mentor Wally Boag)*

"You don't get paid for the hour. You get
paid for the value you bring to the hour."

JIM ROHN
(Best-selling self-help author and speaker)

You must remember that no matter how many hours you put into the podcast, the world will only listen if they are enjoying the audio magic that you are producing.

I would encourage you to not start this journey until you have invested the time needed to identify your chief aim and ultimately why you are wanting to start a podcast. From a technical and cost perspective, anybody can start a podcast with the tools outlined in this book, in fact it's pretty easy. However, where many people will fall short is actually doing it. I would strongly encourage you to not start a podcast unless you are willing to work on it consistently for the next five years without any encouragement or positive feedback because you will be nervous and awkward when you start.

Then over time as a result of listening to your own podcasts and comparing your performances with that of the most successful podcasters you will begin to improve.

"Ideas are easy. Implementation is hard."

GUY KAWASAKI
(An American marketing specialist, author, and Silicon Valley venture capitalist, He was one of the Apple employees originally responsible for marketing their Macintosh computer line in 1984)

"Vision without execution is hallucination."

THOMAS EDISON
(Arguably America's greatest inventor)

This book is designed to teach you the specific steps you must take in order to launch a podcast while starting from absolutely nothing. I encourage you to take your time with it, marinate with it, skip forwards & backwards, laugh with it, and apply the moves - all at your own pace. At The Thrive Time Show, we help countless entrepreneurs like you to achieve thier dreams and throughout the course of this book we are going to be giving you access to the vault of knowledge we have gained from personally helping hundreds of entrepreneurs to launch their own podcasts.

The success of the principles that we will be teaching is not dependent on the niche or topic that you are choosing to podcast about, but rather the diligence with which the principles and steps are applied.

In fact, I have helped business owners and content creators start podcasts in the following niches and more:

1. Accounting
2. Dog Training
3. Entrepreneurship
4. Financial Planning
5. Fitness
6. Functional Medicine and Family Medical Care Physician
7. Loan Officer Training
8. Marketing
9. Home Builder Training
10. Home Health Care
11. Home Title
12. In-Home Cleaning
13. Medical Software
14. Mortgage Banking
15. Music and Entertainment
16. Professional Sports
17. And many more...

Not only have we helped to produce and launch podcasts for others, but we actually produce the daily Thrive Time Business Coach Radio Show which is first aired as a live radio show in select AM radio markets (learn more by visiting www. ThriveTimeShow.com). For this program, I serve as the Executive Producer and as a result I have grown a vast knowledge of what to do, and more importantly what not to do, in order to grow your audience to 10's of thousands of downloads per month. Navigating the technology, organizing guests, creating outlines, and creating a buzz around your podcast is all part of the journey, and the reward is worth it. When you first start out and you are only getting three downloads of each podcast from people you don't know you may begin to ask yourself, "Am I crazy?"

To which you should reply "YES." Because it's the crazy ones who are the ones that believe in themselves and their voice. The crazy ones are the ones who follow through on what they say they are going to do and who do not stop until they get to their destination. You can do this, and I am sincerely excited to hear what you create.

If at any point you feel overwhelmed or have a question, please email us at info@Thrive15.com.

FUN FACTS

Now, known as one of the top earning podcasters on the planet (He brought in $237,193 of income during August of 2017), John Lee Dumas had to start somewhere just like you. Upon leaving the U.S. Army, he enrolled at Roger Williams University School of Law in Bristol, Rhode Island. He then dropped out after only one semester. Dumas then took a took a job working in corporate finance for John Hancock in Boston. He then went to New York City to begin working for a technology startup before leaving to move to San Diego in 2009.

In 2011 he moved back to Maine to start a career in commercial real estate. While getting started in this new career he found himself listening to podcasts and he noticed that none of his favorite podcasts provided content daily, and that's when he had his epiphany. He believed that if he could develop a daily podcast focused on interviewing successful entrepreneurs that would resonate with his target audience of entrepreneurs. He came up with the name, *Entrepreneur On Fire* and decided to call it EOFire for short.

Daily he continued to grind away after first launching his podcast in September 22, 2012. More and more subscribers began to flock to his podcast as a result of his consistent passionate delivery, the daily format, and his ever rising search engine rank (the more podcasts you produce and transcribe the higher you will rise in Google search results) he then created the book called, *Podcast Launch,* which he published in the Amazon bookstore. In 2013 fueled by the success of both his book and his podcast he launched the Podcaster's Paradise (which is a community of podcasters).

"If you are not willing to commit to diligently working to achieve your dream for 5 years without any positive feedback, don't start a business."

CLAY CLARK
Former U.S. Small Business Administration Entrepreneur of the Year and the founder of multiple multi-million dollar businesses - DJConnection.com, EITRLounge.com, EpicPhotos. com, MakeYourLifeEpic.com, etc.

"You must be the pig at breakfast and not just the chicken. The pig gives his life for the breakfast, whereas the chicken just lays an egg. You must give your life to your business."

DR. ZOELLNER
(The CEO of ThriveTimeShow.com and the founder / partner of multiple multi-million dollar businesses - Z66AA.com. DrZoellner.com, BankRegent.com, http://RockinZRanchOK.com/, http://DrZZZs.com/, http://www.ZoellnerMedicalGroup.com/, etc...)

FUN FACT

The following entrepreneurs and world-leaders succeeded despite not having a college degree and access to institutional wealth:

Abraham Lincoln

Despite not having earned the respect of his peers by obtaining a college degree, he went on to become a lawyer and president of the United States. Because he chose to be self-taught, he never did stop learning until the day of his death.

1832 - Lost job and was defeated for state legislature.

1833 - Failed in business.

1843 - Lost his attempt to be nominated for Congress.

1848 - Lost renomination for Congress.

1849 - Rejected in his attempt to become land officer.

1854 - Defeated for U.S. Senate.

1856 - Defeated for nomination for Vice President.

1848 - Defeated for U.S. Senate.

Amadeo Peter Giannini

Despite not knowing what he was doing because he didn't have a master's degree from a fancy business college, he went on to become the multi-millionaire founder of Bank of America after dropping out of high school.

Andrew Carnegie

Despite being an elementary school dropout, this man went on to become the world's wealthiest man during his lifetime. Amazing, since he couldn't possibly have known what he was doing because he didn't have a college degree.

Andrew Jackson

This guy went on to become an attorney, a U.S. president, a general, a judge, and a congressman despite being home-schooled and having no formal education at all.

Anne Beiler

The "Princess of Pretzels" went on to start Auntie Anne's Pretzels and to become a millionaire, despite having dropped out of high school. I bet she's disappointed she missed out on the once-in-a-lifetime experiences that so many college graduates with $100,000 of debt enjoyed.

Ansel Adams

I don't know if you are into world-famous photographers or not, but if you are, you know that Ansel Adams became arguably the best photographer in the world despite not graduating from a college of liberal arts. I wonder how he even knew to take the lens cap off of his camera without a college degree.

Barry Diller

This dude may be a billionaire and Hollywood mogul who founded Fox Broadcasting Company, but I am not impressed with him because he does not have a college degree.

Benjamin Franklin

This guy might have invented the Franklin stove, lightning rods, bifocals, and other assorted inventions while working as a founding father of the United States, but I can tell you that he had a hole in his soul where his degree should have been.

Billy Joe (Red) McCombs

Red became a billionaire, but did he have a degree? No. And that is exactly why he doesn't get invited to any of those fancy alumni gatherings, which he would be too busy to attend anyway because he's off counting his money. Seriously, if he started counting the billions of dollars he made by founding Clear Channel media, he would never finish.

Bill Gates

He started that little company that Steve Jobs fought. That's it. And he can take his $53 billion and go buy boats, houses and stuff, but he can't buy the memories that he missed out on making by not graduating from college.

Coco Chanel

She may have a perfume that bears her name, but I am not impressed with her because she doesn't have a degree.

Colonel Harlan Sanders

This guy dropped out of elementary school and all he knew about was chicken. Sure he made millions, but I didn't truly have respect for him until he finally earned that law degree by correspondence.

Dave Thomas

Every time I pull into Wendy's to enjoy a delicious snack wrap, I find myself thinking about what a complete waste of talent Dave was. He could have had trillions of dollars if only he had earned a degree.

David Geffen

Like a true loser, he dropped out of college after completing only one year. My, his parents must be disappointed. I feel bad just writing about this billionaire founder of Geffen Records and co-founder of DreamWorks.

David Green

David, oh David. I bet you feel bad about your billions and spend everyday living in regret because you do not have a college degree. I know that you took $600 and famously turned that into billions as the founder of Hobby Lobby, but you could have been a good attorney or a bureaucrat or a politician we all could watch argue to an empty room on C-SPAN.

David Karp

This guy's last name should be carp, because this bottom feeder obviously will never amount to anything – well, except being the multi-millionaire founder of Tumblr. If he hadn't dropped out of school at age 15, I would respect him more.

David Neeleman

This guy started a little airline (JetBlue) to compensate for his lack of a degree. I don't even feel safe on the world's most profitable airline because its founder doesn't have a degree.

David Oreck

David Oreck truly had a career that sucked. This college dropout and multi-millionaire founder of the Oreck vacuum company created vacuums that have sucked the dirt out of carpets for years.

Debbi Fields

Oh, so sad. Little Debbie, the founder Mrs. Fields Chocolate Chippery, never knew the pride that one could feel upon earning a college degree.

DeWitt Wallace

DeWitt may have founded Reader's Digest, but I'm sure that he could not truly enjoy reading in an intelligent way because he never earned his college degree.

EDITOR'S NOTE: It took Clay three weeks to alphabetize this list of college dropouts because he doesn't have a degree.

Dustin Moskovitz

Dustin is credited as being one of the founders of that little company called Facebook that only moms, dads, cousins, kids, adults, and humans use. I bet he wishes he had stayed in school at Harvard.

Frank Lloyd Wright

Frank may have become the most famous architect of all time, but I cannot respect a man who never attended high school.

Frederick Henry Royce

Okay, so a Rolls-Royce is a symbol of automotive excellence for many people, but this guy had to have been compensating for the fact that he knew nothing about anything because he was an elementary school dropout.

George Eastman

Perhaps you are not old enough to know about the Kodak brand that used to control the world as part of the Illuminati. How George founded this little company despite dropping out of high school is beyond me. It's so sad.

H. Wayne Huizenga

Wayne is a beautiful man and founder of WMX Garbage Company, and he also helped launch the Blockbuster Video chain. Good for him! Because without a degree, he was basically screwed.

Henry Ford

Okay, so I've mentioned this guy in the book, but without a college degree, you can bet this billionaire founder of the Ford Motor Company was never respected by his father-in-law.

Henry J. Kaiser

This multimillionaire and founder of Kaiser Aluminum didn't even graduate from high school. Think about it. Without a diploma, there was no way he could have become one of those pharmaceutical reps who delivers sales presentations and catering to doctors every day in exchange for their allegiance in writing prescriptions for the drugs the rep is peddling.

Hyman Golden

This guy spent his whole life making drinks and millions. I bet you the founder of Snapple lived a life of regret while endlessly chanting to himself, "Why me? No Degree. Why me? No degree."

Ingvar Kamprad

I believe IKEA's business model is in jeopardy. Their founder has no degree. The lines of customers are now so long that no one even wants to go there anymore. Oh...and he's dyslexic.

Isaac Merrit Singer

This sewing machine inventor dropped out of high school because he was spending all his time sewing. I am SEW sorry for him.

Jack Crawford Taylor

Although this man did serve honorably as a World War II fighter pilot for the Navy, I wonder what he is going to fall back on if his Enterprise Rent-a-Car venture fails.

James Cameron

Avatar...overrated. Titanic...overrated. Winning an Oscar... overrated. But what did you expect from a director, writer, and film guy who dropped out of college?

Jay Van Andel

A billionaire co-founder of Amway...not impressive without a degree. He does not know the meaning of life.

Jerry Yang

Who even uses Yahoo anyway, other than the 20% of the world that does? This guy threw it all away and dropped out of a PhD program. I bet you he can't even spell "Yahoo!"

Jimmy Dean

Food is so simple. You grow it. You eat it. You raise it. You kill it and eat it. How complex could it be if a man was able to start this multi-million dollar company after dropping out of high school at age 16?

Jimmy Iovine

This man grew up as the son of a secretary and a longshoreman. However, at the age of 19 his ambition had become his mission. Obsessed with making records, he began working as a studio professional around the year of 1972 when a friend of his got him a job cleaning a recording studio. Soon he found himself recording with John Lennon, Bruce Springsteen and other top artists. In 1973 he landed a full-time job on the staff of the New York recording studio, Record Plant where he worked on Meat Loaf's *Bat Out of Hell* album and Springsteen's *Born to Run* album. He went on to be involved in the production of more than 250 million albums. In 2006, Iovine teamed with Dr. Dre to found Beats Electronics. This company was purchased by Apple for $3 billion in May 2014. I hope he goes on to be successful despite not having a degree.

John D. Rockefeller Sr.

So my son and I did name our Great Pyrenees dog after this man, but we wouldn't have named a human after him, because although Rockefeller became the wealthiest man in the world, he didn't have a degree and I judge him for this.

John Mackey

The guy who founded Whole Foods Market, the millennial mecca of the great organic panic that has swept our nation, enrolled and dropped out of college six times. Now he's stuck working at a grocery store in a dead-end job.

John Paul DeJoria

This man is the billionaire co-founder of John Paul Mitchell Systems and dude who also founded Patron Spirits. That's it. That's all he's accomplished. No degree.

Joyce C. Hall

This guy spent his whole life writing apology cards to his family for shaming them by not graduating from college. When he wasn't doing that, he was running that little company he founded called Hallmark.

Kemmons Wilson

This dude started the Holiday Inn chain after dropping out of high school. But then what? What's he doing now? Well he's not buying huge amounts of college logo apparel and running down to the college football stadium eight Saturdays per year while talking about the good old days with his frat brothers because he doesn't have a degree.

Kevin Rose

This dude dropped out of college and started a company called Digg.com. I'm not impressed with his millions. I just want to see that degree.

Kirk Kerkorian

I did see a Boyz II Men concert at the Mirage Resorts that this guy owns. But, I have never stayed at the Mandalay Bay resort that he owns in Las Vegas more than once. It's good that he owns MGM Studios because the closest he'll ever come to a degree is if he makes a movie about himself getting a degree. He dropped out of school in 8th grade.

Larry Ellison

Larry is the billionaire co-founder of Oracle software company and he is a man who dropped out of two different colleges. Oh, the regret he must feel.

Leandro Rizzuto

This guy spent his time building Conair and that was it. Now, just because he is billionaire, does he think we should respect him even though he does not have a degree?

Leslie Wexner

My wife buys stuff from the L Brands (the global retail empire that owns Victoria's Secret, Bath & Body Works, and Limited), but I am still not impressed with the fact that this law school dropout started a billion-dollar brand with $5,000.

Mark Ecko

If you are one of those people who has success based upon the success you have, then I suppose Mark Ecko is impressive. This multi-millionaire is the founder of Mark Ecko Enterprises, but he dropped out of college.

Mary Kay Ash

I feel like Prince should have written a song about the pink Cadillacs that Mary Kay was famous for giving to her top sales reps. But I am not impressed with her because she didn't attend college.

Michael Dell

He may be the billionaire founder of Dell Computers, but he probably doesn't feel like a billionaire since he never experienced the college joys of drunken music festivals and regrettable one-night stands.

Milton Hershey

Like I always say, "If you drop out of 4th grade you are going to spend your entire life making chocolate." That is what the founder of Hershey's Milk Chocolate did.

Rachael Ray

Her happiness and genuine love for people and food makes me mad because without formal culinary arts training, this Food Network cooking show star and food industry entrepreneur is just a sham.

Ray Kroc

He dropped out of high school, founded McDonald's, and spent his whole life saying, "Do you want fries with that?" So sad.

Richard Branson

So he's the billionaire founder of Virgin Records, Virgin Atlantic Airways, Virgin Mobile, and more. But did he graduate from high school? No. He dropped out of his high school at the age of 16. So sad.

Richard Schulze

He's the Best Buy founder, but he did not attend college. Doesn't he know that the investment in a college degree is truly the Best Buy you can ever make?

Rob Kalin

Rob is the founder of Etsy, but who even uses Etsy other than all of the humans on earth? This dude flunked out of high school, then he enrolled in art school. He created a fake student ID for MIT so he could take the courses that he wanted. His professors were so impressed by his scam that they actually helped him get into NYU. Rob, you have to get it together.

Ron Popeil

The dude who is constantly talking about dehydrating your meat and the multimillionaire founder of Ronco did not graduate from college.

Rush Limbaugh

This guy irritates half of America every day for three hours per day. I believe that this multi-millionaire media maven and radio talk show host would be more liked if he had graduated from a liberal arts college and would have purchased a Prius pre-loaded with left-wing bumper stickers.

Russell Simmons

This guy is co-founder of Def Jam records and the founder of the Russell Simmons Music Group. He's also the founder of Phat Farm fashions and a bestselling author. He didn't graduate from college because he claims to have been too busy introducing rap and hip hop music to the planet.

S. Daniel Abraham

This man founded Slim-Fast without even having a degree in nutrition. Outside of the millions of people who use his products every day to lose weight, who is going to trust him with their health since he doesn't even have a college degree?

Sean John Combs

The man who is en route to becoming the first hip-hop billionaire in part because of his ownership in the Ciroc Vodka brand did not graduate from college because he was spending his time discovering and promoting Mary J. Blige, The Notorious B.I.G., Jodeci, and other R&B stars. If this man ever wants to become truly successful, he will go back to Howard University and get that degree.

Shawn Fanning

This is the music industry-killing devil who created Napster and went on to become a multi-millionaire. If he would have stayed in college, he would have learned to follow the rules.

Simon Cowell

This famous TV producer, judger of people, American Idol, The X Factor, and Britain's Got Talent star dropped out of high school. He has been negative ever since. He obviously needs a college degree to calm him down because I've never met a college graduate who is mean.

Steve Jobs

This hippie dropped out of college and frankly, his little Apple company barely made it.

Steve Madden

Steve dropped out of college and now spends his entire life making shoes. He may be worth millions, but I'm sure that you and I are not impressed.

Steve Wozniak

Okay, so I did know that Steve Jobs co-founded Apple with this guy and both of them became billionaires, but they experienced what I call a "hollow success" because they did not take the time to earn a college degree.

Theodore Waitt

This man became a billionaire by selling a PC to every human possible during the 1990s. He may have co-founded Gateway computers but without a degree, how will he ever experience true success? I bet that he regrets not having a degree.

Thomas Edison

Tommy Boy wasn't smart enough to graduate from high school, yet he was crazy enough to invent the modern light bulb, recorded audio, and recorded video. I am never impressed with crazy people who don't graduate from high school.

Tom Anderson

This dude co-founded MySpace after dropping out of high school. He made his millions, but who ever had a MySpace account anyway?

Ty Warner

I think the only thing weirder than collecting Beanie Babies is to have invented them. To cover up this weird Beanie Babies fixation, this billionaire has gone on to purchase real estate. College would have taught him that it is not normal for an adult to be interested in stuffed animals.

Vidal Sassoon

This dude founded Vidal Sassoon after dropping out of high school. Had he graduated from college, I'm sure his product would have been better.

W. Clement Stone

This guy started the billion-dollar insurance company called Combined Insurance. He then went on to start *Success* Magazine and write books to keep himself busy because he felt so bad that he didn't have a college degree.

Wally "Famous" Amos

This man did not graduate from high school and spent almost his entire working career making people fat by selling them Famous Amos cookies. If he had graduated from college, he might have invented a product that makes people thin and able to live forever while tasting good, you know, like carrots.

Walt Disney

This struggling entrepreneur who never really figured it out co-founded the Walt Disney Company with his brother Roy. He didn't even graduate from high school, which is probably why he spent his entire life drawing cartoons.

Wolfgang Puck

Okay, so my wife and I buy his soup. Okay, so I have eaten at his restaurant a few times. But I can't respect a man who dropped out of high school at the age of 14. Yes, he's opened up 16 restaurants and 80 bistros. So what? Respecting people like this sets a bad example for kids because not everyone can go on to become a successful entrepreneur, but everyone can incur $100,000 of student loan debt before finding a soul-sucking job doing something they don't like in exchange for a paycheck.

WARNING

Marshall is about to teach you specifically what you need to do to create a successful podcast, and after he does this, it will be 100% your fault or your credit whether you fail or succeed. Now is your last chance to put a checkbox by the excuse you can use to justify why you did not succeed as a podcaster:

☐ **I DID NOT SUCCEED AS A PODCASTER BECAUSE I DID NOT KNOW HOW**

☐ **I DID NOT SUCCEED AS A PODCASTER BECAUSE I RAN OUT OF TIME**

☐ **I DID NOT SUCCEED AS A PODCASTER BECAUSE I DID NOT HAVE THE MONEY NEEDED**

FUN FACTS

"The average American loses almost $400 per year to gambling. According to one study, 27.1 percent of gamblers who reported spending over 5 percent of their gross family income monthly, also report experiencing serious problems because of their gambling habit, including health problems, high debts, financial issues, or guilt and other negative emotions.

According to the Bureau of Labor Statistics, the average American consumer dedicates 1 percent of all their spending to alcohol, or about $1 of every $100!

14 percent of Americans' incomes are spent on cigarettes, rounding out to roughly one-seventh of their total income.

the International Health, Racquet, & Sportsclub Association released a statistic stating that gyms sell memberships with the expectation that only 18 percent of people will use their membership on a consistent basis.

According to CNN, Americans spent $66.5 billion on lottery tickets in 2011, an increase of nearly 10 percent from the year before. The odds of getting struck by lightning in your lifetime, being injured by a toilet this year, getting killed by a shark, and killed by an asteroid or comet are much more likely (than that of winning the lottery.)

According to a recent survey of American workers by Accounting Principals, Americans who regularly buy coffee throughout the week spend on average, $1,092 on coffee annually."

KATHERINE MUNIZ
20 ways Americans are blowing their money
USA Today

https://www.usatoday.com/story/money/personalfinance/2014/03/24/20-ways-we-blow-our-money/6826633/

"What gets scheduled gets done."

LEE COCKERELL
(The former Executive Vice President of Walt Disney World Resorts who once managed over 40,000 cast members)

FUN FACT

"On average, American adults are watching five hours and four minutes of television per day. The bulk of that — about four and a half hours of it — is live television, which is television watched when originally broadcast. Thirty minutes more comes via DVR."

JOHN KOBLIN
How Much Do We Love TV? Let Us Count the Ways
New York Times

https://www.nytimes.com/2016/07/01/business/media/nielsen-survey-media-viewing.html

"A recent report from Nielsen found that Generation X, or people between the ages of 35 to 49, spend almost seven hours a week on social media.

MAHITA GAJANAN
Middle-Aged Americans Spend More Time on Social Media than Millennials

http://fortune.com/2017/01/25/social-media-millennials-generation-x/

"If you get stuck and you don't know what to do, just book your tickets for our next in-person Thrive Time Show 2-Day Interactive Business Workshop. These events attract people from all over the world and we have a scholarship available to help people just like you if you can't afford the tickets right now. I grew up poor and I know what it's like to not have access to mentors. But my friend, you now have access to a team and we sincerely want to help you, but you must take the first step. Book your tickets today at www. ThriveTimeShow.com."

CLAY CLARK
(Father of fice kids and the host of the daily ThriveTime Business Coach radio show.)

"Ninety-nine percent of the failures come from people who have the habit of making excuses."

GEORGE WASHINGTON CARVER
(A man who was born into slavery and who went on to help economically liberate African Americans as a result of his endless and obsessive study of peanuts and sweet potatoes. Because of his tireless research and efforts African Americans were able to return the much needed nutrients to their farm land which had been ruined after years of planting cotton on the same pieces of land over and over.)

"If you cannot save money, the seeds of greatness are not in you."

W. CLEMENT STONE
(Best-selling self-help author and the founder of the Combined Insurance Company of America which sold accident and health insurance coverage)

"My wife and I turned off our air-conditioning and shared a car while I worked three jobs and she worked two in order to finance the advertising for our first big success DJConnection.com. Holding jobs at Applebee's, Target and DirecTV at the same time was tough. However, it would have been tougher to have been content to live a life of mediocrity because of buying into the excuse that "I couldn't afford to advertise" and to invest in my business. Life is all about trade-offs.

What are you willing to trade off to become successful?"

CLAY CLARK
(A guy who made the neccessary sacrifice so that his business would be successful.)

"People who are unable to motivate themselves must be content with mediocrity, no matter how impressive their other talents."

ANDREW CARNEGIE
(One of the world's wealthiest people who started working at the age of 13 to help support his family's financial needs)

"People around you, constantly under the pull of thier emotions, change their ideas by the day or by the hour, depending on their mood. You must never assume that what people say or do in a particular moment is a statement of their permanent desires"

ROBERT GREENE
(Best-selling author of Mastery, 48 Laws of Power, and other titles)

FUN FACT:
YOUR SMARTPHONE IS MAKING YOU DUMB

"Imagine that after a routine medical exam your doctor delivers some devastating news: Since your last checkup, your cognitive performance has plummeted. Your ability to connect with others has eroded. And your memory for everyday events is no longer operating as it once did.

As it turns out, there is a cure and it won't cost you a penny. The treatment is simple: All that's required is that you put away your smartphone.

Few of us will have this conversation with our doctors. But perhaps we should. Over the last few years, scientists have begun studying the way cell phones affect the human experience. And the early results are alarming.

RON FRIEDMAN PH.D.
Is Your Smartphone Making You Dumb?
USA Today

https://www.psychologytoday.com/blog/glue/201501/is-your-smartphone-making-you-dumb

"We need to re-create boundaries. When you carry a digital gadget that creates a virtual link to the office, you need to create a virtual boundary that didn't exist before."

DANIEL GOLEMAN
(His 1995 book, Emotional Intelligence was on the New York Times best-seller list for a year-and-a-half. He received a Career Achievement Award for journalism from the American Psychological Association)

"I quit because I wasn't getting any traction." People who make this statement are weak-ass. Every successful entrepreneur I've ever met when through hell and back to find their path to success. You must refuse right now not to quit no matter how challenging the situation and no matter how long it takes to make a profit or you should not start."

CLAY CLARK
*(Former U.S. Small Business Administration
Entrepreneur of the Year and the co-founder of 5
human kids)*

FUN FACTS

"Bill Gates may have founded Microsoft in 1975, but it took him nearly six years to land his big contract with IBM. Have you ever worked on something without traction for six years?

Apple was started in 1976, but it really didn't "gain traction" until the creation of the Macintosh in 1984 (8 years later). How would you feel if you had been working on something that didn't show much progress after 8 years?

Google was started in 1996, yet by 1999 still almost nobody had heard of the struggling search engine. Oh, by the way...the company was originally called BackRub. I wonder what would have happened if they had refused to change the name? I wonder if they ever felt stress? Read the true story behind the original Google's first name - http://www.businessinsider.com/the-true-story-behind-googles-first-name-backrub-2015-10

When Mark Zuckerberg started this company during his sophomore year at Harvard he originally called it "Facemash" as a way to distract himself from losing a girlfriend. As of 2005, Facebook had posted a yearly net loss of $3.63 million dollars. I wonder if he felt discouraged? I wonder if they ever felt stress?

Amazon was founded by Jeff Bezos in 1994 using his life savings and the life savings of his Mom and Dad's $300,000 retirement. However, in 1999 despite having sales of $1.6 billion, Amazon.com posted a whopping loss of $719 million. In 2003 after having been in business of 9 years, Amazon.com finally posted a profit. How stressed out would you be if you had spent your entire life savings and had built a billion dollar business that just publically declared a loss of $719 million?

Ted Turner's father literally (this is not an analogy or an exaggeration) told him that he was disappointed by him and then he killed himself. Then Ted went out and leveraged his life savings to buy a small UHF TV 17 station in 1970. Before 1980, fueled by his desire to prove his deceased father wrong, Ted had produced enough revenue and profits to by the Atlanta Hawks, the Atlanta Braves and Superstation TV 17. I wonder how bad Ted felt when his father blamed him for his suicide? However, he chose to turn his bitterness into betterness.

When Elon Musk took over the Tesla company founded by Martin Eberhard and Marc Tarpenning the company was losing money and had been losing money since 2003. Despite Musk's hard work and genius, the company continued to lose money until 2013. I wonder how stressed out Elon Musk must have felt with his life's savings and his reputation on the line?"

NOT A VALID EXCUSE
☐ I DIDN'T HAVE ANY SUPPORT

FUN FACT

Email us to info@Thrive15.com and book your tickets to the next ThriveTimeShow.com in-person 2-day interactive business workshop and we will teach you first hand everything you need to know about podcasting and starting a successful business. We will have one of our team members work with you through the technical aspects of setting up and recording your podcast. We also have a scholarship available, so it is literally your choice as to whether you will take advantage of this resource or not.

CHAPTER 1

WHY START A PODCAST?

LET'S BEGIN. FIRST, WE NEED TO ESTABLISH WHY A PODCAST IS THE BEST PLATFORM FOR YOU.

There's a variety of ways to get your ideas and thoughts out amongst the masses of humanity, but podcasting is special. With super niche content, people grow attached to a show or program. Look at the mob of fans for the Entreprenuers on Fire Podcast, or the fantastic following of The Tim Ferriss Show. Podcasting has a variety of reasons that make it far better than a blog or radio program for your content, so let's get into them.

REASON 1: MONETIZE A PODCAST

In my experience, about 50% of those that want to start a podcast are wanting to do so because they would rather earn an income from podcasting than from their current job. Podcasts are wonderful because anybody can start one as long as you are sincerely passionate about your subject and are committed to knowing 10 times more about your subject than the average person. Furthermore, anybody can make money from them - if you're willing to hustle and to remain consistent. Here's how:

"If you aren't willing to invest the time needed to become an expert in your given subject then don't waste your time creating a podcast. Everyone knows when the presenter is not prepared and does not know their material. You owe it to your audience to prepare and if you are not willing to do that then you need to avoid podcasting."

CLAY CLARK
*(Former U.S. Small Business Administration
Entrepreneur of the Year and the co-founder of 5
human kids)*

"In the future, the great division will be between those who have trained themselves to handle these complexities and those who are overwhelmed by them -- those who can acquire skills and discipline their minds and those who are irrevocably distracted by all the media around them and can never focus enough to learn."

ROBERT GREENE
(Best-selling author of Mastery)

Advertisement

This allows mere mortals like you and me (although you are far more beautiful than me) to create an audience that is interested in a specific niche or topic that other companies and brands are interested in reaching. Typically, this is also known as sponsorship. These companies and brands want to leverage the work you have put into growing your audience and wish to target your group of raving fans. So if you have started a pet care podcast that addresses the tips and tricks for effective pet care, and you grow your audience to 10s of thousands of downloads, then a likely ideal sponsor for your podcast might be PetSmart because their customers are the same as your audience. Usually this takes the form of a pre-roll advertisement (audio commercial before the podcast), or a mid roll advertisement (audio commercial 60% of the way through the duration of the podcast episode). We'll talk more about that later.

FUN FACT

To calculate exactly how much money a successful and often downloaded podcast can make you go to www.midroll.com

Affiliate Commisions

You can actually reach out to the brands and companies that you like and frequently use to become an affiliate for their product or service. Over time, you will develop a relationship with your audience – one which will position you as an authority figure for other resources for the audience to use. By recommending that your audience check out a specific company and take advantage of an exclusive offer, certain companies will actually pay you for every customer that claims the offer.

AMPLE EXAMPLE

Top podcasters like EOFire.com and FourHourWorkWeek.com earn tremendous amounts of income as a result of their affiliate relationship with popular brands with brands such as Libsyn.com, Wordpress.com, FourSigmatic.com, and MeUndies.com.

Selling a Product

Utilizing your new podcast can be a great way to educate your audience about a product or service that you offer. The podcast should not become a "homer" (someone who shows blind loyalty to a team or organization, typically ignoring any shortcomings or faults they have) for your product or service, but it can be undoubtedly a perfect platform on which to talk about it.

AMPLE EXAMPLE

The best-selling author Malcolm Gladwell has created numerous books which he on occasion will promote through his podcast – http://revisionisthistory.com/. However, his podcast is so good that you as a listener want to buy his books – http://gladwell.com/

REASON 2: SEARCH ENGINE OPTIMIZATION (SEO)

This is the most underrated and underutilized purpose for creating a podcast. Coming up on the first page of Google IS A GAME-CHANGING AND LIFE-CHANGING FACTOR THAT WILL CAUSE YOUR BUSINESS AND PODCAST TO THRIVE (if your product is good). In the past 10 years of my life, I have never seen or heard someone say, "I don't want to go with any of these results for businesses on Page 1 of Google. Let me go to Page 2 to peruse others." No, stop it. The best place to hide things is on Page 2 of Google, because nobody ever looks there.

FUN FACT

"92 percent of Internet users (now) search using search engines on a daily basis"

Who Uses Search Engines? 92% of Adult U.S. Internet Users [Study]
https://searchenginewatch.com/sew/study/2101282/search-engines-92-adult-internet-users-study

SEO Crash Course

To begin, here's a quick crash course on search engine optimization (SEO) that your current web developer will never tell you. It's simple, and you can understand it enough to become an SEO ninja. The following four variables will impact your search engine ranking.

1. **The Most Original HTML Content about a given keyword or subject**
   Much like why Wikipedia is top in Google for the word "dog" – it has the most content about dogs...

FUN FACT

HTML (Hypertext Markup Language) is the set of markup symbols or codes inserted in a file intended for display on a World Wide Web browser page. The markup tells the Web browser how to display a Web page's words and images for the user

2. **The Most Google Reviews for an optimized Google My Business Listing**
Get more 5x more reviews than your competitors, and you will win.

3. **A Mobile Compliant Website**
Your website must work well on smartphones. Pass or fail.

"Mobile is changing the world. Today, everyone has smartphones with them, constantly communicating and looking for information. In many countries, the number of smartphones has surpassed the number of personal computers; having a mobile-friendly website has become a critical part of having an online presence.

If you haven't made your website mobile-friendly, you should. The majority of users coming to your site are likely to be using a mobile device.

If you don't know if your website is mobile-friendly, take the Mobile Friendly Test now!

If you used content management software like Wordpress to build you website, Check out our guide to customize your website software. If you don't use such software, consider hiring a web developer.

We have a checklist of things to care about when doing so.

If you're technical enough to do it yourself, check our Mobile SEO Guide."

MR. GOOGLE
https://developers.google.com/search/mobile-sites/

4. **The Most Google Compliant Site following the canonical rules will rank the highest in the Google search engine**
There is a list of 35+ items like meta descriptions, XML sitemaps, horizontal navigation bars, focus keywords, HTML sitemaps, page load speeds that you will need to optimize. Our team will run a FREE diagnostic search engine compliance test on your website if you just email your web address to info@Thrive15.com.

FUN FACT

A sitemap is a model of a website's content designed to help both users and search engines navigate the site. A sitemap can be a hierarchical list of pages (with links) organized by topic, an organization chart, or an XML document that provides instructions to search engine crawl bots. 1) The HTML sitemap is designed to be viewed by humans 2) The XML sitemap is designed to be viewed by search engine crawl bots.

A Web crawler, sometimes called a spider, is an Internet bot that systematically browses the World Wide Web, typically for the purpose of Web indexing (web spidering). Indexing refers to sorting websites based upon which sites are the most relevant for the users who are using a web browser to search for the answers they are looking for.

"To learn everything that you will ever need to learn about search engines go to www.ThriveTimeShow.com and download our Amazon best-selling book, *Start Here,* for FREE today."

CLAY CLARK
(A man who is thankful that persistence is a good substitute for talent and skill)

As a byproduct of your diligent podcasting, you create the most original content for a keyword or a subject. Because the nature of a successful podcast episode is talking about a topic or niche, all of this audio can then be transcribed into glorious text using an affordable transcription service like EndQuote.net. In order to help you do this, Clay Clark actually teamed up with a Massachusets Institute of Technology graduate (Chalen Miller) to create Endquote.net, which is the world's fastest and most affordable transcription service. TRY IT TODAY. YOUR FIRST TRANSCRIPTION IS 100% FREE!

Now, the other factors are important too, so if you'd like to learn more about them and get the checklist for how to optimize your site (that we use for our own sites), you can get the *Start Here* book that we've written by going to www.Amazon.com and searching "business growth" or you can download it for free at www.ThrivetimeShow.com.

REASON 3: ACCESS WHENEVER YOU WANT

One of the most fantastic benefits of podcasting is the accessibility to your content whenever the audience wants it! You used to have to wait for your favorite show or radio program to come on, and God forbid something came up in your schedule. There was no replay or skip ahead. You had to be in front of the radio or television ready to listen as the program was streamed to you.

FUN FACT

Podcasting continues to rise, with monthly listeners growing from 21% to 24% year over year.

The audience for podcasts continues to be predominately 18-54, and leans slightly male.

The podcast listener remains an affluent, educated consumer – and one that is becoming increasingly more likely to gravitate to ad-free or ad-light subscription experiences.

Clicking on a podcast to listen to it immediately (either streamed or via progressive download) is the dominant paradigm for listening, though 27% do subscribe to podcasts.

Subscribers tend to have been podcast consumers for longer than non-subscribers, consume more podcasts, and are more likely to use their smartphone as their primary podcast player.

While "home" continues to be the most often named location for podcast listening, the vehicle is a strong second.

Most podcast consumers listen to most of the podcast episodes they download, and the vast majority listen to at least most of each episode.

http://www.edisonresearch.com/the-podcast-consumer-2017/

Now, you can access podcast content anywhere, and from any device. Studies have shown that anywhere from 50% – 80% of people that are accessing the internet are doing so from their mobile smartphones.

With the decreasing cost of technology, smartphones are becoming more available to people to use for a variety of activities, including listening to podcasts. Not only are podcasts available through traditional computers, but your smartphone, your iPad, your Apple Watch, and your tablet all can download and access podcasts. No more waiting for a specific time of day to hear your favorite host talk about vegan cooking or your favorite sports anchor rant about an overpaid athlete.

FUN FACT

"...80% of connected consumers report using a mobile phone to access the internet on a weekly basis..."

Forbes
5 Stats You Need to Know About Connected Consumers in 2017, Euromonitor International's 2016 Global Consumer Trends Survey

REASON 4: CONNECT WITH YOUR AUDIENCE

There was a client that we worked with years ago that owned a bridal boutique where future brides could come try on dresses and drink champagne and revel in the excitement of being a bride-to-be. This business owner wanted a way to connect further with the brides that came into her store when she discovered podcasting. There is a large difference between podcasting and writing a blog. With podcasts, you have the opportunity to more emotionally and empathically connect with your audience in a way that blogging and the written word cannot. You are literally in the listener's ear talking to them almost as if it were a personal conversation you are sharing. For companies and business owners looking for a way to further connect with their customers, creating a podcast audience is a great way to achieve that.

"Getting an audience is hard. Sustaining an audience is hard. It demands a consistency of thought, of purpose, and of action over a long period of time."

BRUCE SPRINGSTEEN
(Springsteen's recordings have included both commercially accessible rock albums and more somber folk-oriented works. His most successful studio albums, Born to Run (1975) and Born in the U.S.A. (1984) find pleasures in the struggles of daily American life. He has sold more than 120 million records worldwide and more than 64 million records in the United States, making him one of the world's best-selling artists of all time. He has earned numerous awards for his work, including 20 Grammy Awards, two Golden Globes, and an Academy Award as well as being inducted into both the Songwriters Hall of Fame and the Rock And Roll Hall Of Fame in 1999)

REASON 5: IT'S FREE FOR LISTENERS

One of the most important benefits to listeners of your podcast is that it's FREE for them! Podcasts can grow an audience very quickly because of the low barrier to access new and exciting podcasts every day. So as your preferences and interests change, so can your list of podcasts that you regularly listen to and download.

REASON 6: BECOME AN EXPERT

An exciting part of regular podcasting is that you will build a relationship with your listeners. If you are providing quality content that is both interesting, relevant, and helpful for your listener base, they will begin to see you as an expert in your specific niche or subject. This is powerful for those that are looking to build a following for a niche that might not otherwise receive widespread publicity. Your listeners will value your consistency in how frequently you post just as much as your quality. Many times, podcasters focus entirely on the quality and forget about the quantity and consistency of which you are posting. Others will simply produce content without preparation at all. Make sure that you take time to prepare valuable content for your audience and follow through on your commitment for how regularly you tell your listeners they can find new content.

REASON 7: EXTEND YOUR REACH

The last reason why podcasting can be an effective and fun tool for you is that it allows you to become vaguely famous beyond your current geographical reach. When you publish your podcast online, it will reach far and wide across the world, accessible by those in Kyrgyzstan, Djibouti, and even Iowa (they now have the internet too). Now you will not be limited by the region you live in or broadcast from.

We were launching a podcast for a physician a couple years ago and he committed to recording and producing 3 podcasts every week for his private practice. It took him until about podcast episode #100 and a couple guest features on other podcasts before he began receiving emails from listeners that were halfway across the country. These emails said things like "I just bought my plane ticket, and I'm excited for my appointment in two days."

He had no idea why people across the country were booking appointments with him until he asked how they had heard about him, to which they replied, "Well, you talked about my condition at length on your podcast episode so I wanted to learn more." His podcast had taken off in his niche across the country and he was viewed as an expert by those not even located near him.

FUN FACT

Visit www.RevolutionHealth.org to learn more about our business coaching client and friend, Doctor Chad Edwards.

CHAPTER 2

DEFINING YOUR PODCAST

The first step in launching your podcast is to define the niche and topic you wish to talk about. If you are launching a podcast for search engine optimization purposes, then your topic will be your keyword or company's product or services. Having a clear idea for what you will talk about will provide you direction for where your podcast will grow.

> "Best buyers buy more, buy faster, and buy more often than other buyers. These are your ideal clients. Have a special effort dedicated to just the dream clients."

CHET HOLMES
(Best-selling author of The Ultimate Sales Machine and the former business partner of Charlie Munger, Warren Buffett's billionaire partner that no one has ever heard about)

DEFINE YOUR TOPIC

You do not need to have all of the answers in order to start podcasting, but you must have a general direction. When Thomas Jefferson (former US president for you history buffs, check out your $20 bill) negotiated the Louisiana Purchase, he didn't have a map detailing every route for explorers William Clark & Meriwether Lewis to navigate to the Pacific Ocean. But he did say, "West." Get the general direction for what you want the podcast to communicate and make corrections along the way. Part of the battle is constant improvement.

In order to position yourself as an expert in any given subject, you must ask yourself, "What is it that I know 10x more about than everyone else?" If you think about it, you don't go to your auto mechanic for marriage counseling and you don't ask the waiter how to get rid of chickenpox. However, we do go to experts that have a vast knowledge beyond our understanding of a subject for advice and guidance.

Another direction is to become the Wikipedia of a given subject. This entails providing the most extensive knowledge about a given subject and to research and organize the information for your listeners. While you don't need to be an expert on the subject, this might involve you incorporating other experts and sources of information into your program. This has become a popular format for podcasters in many different niches.

> "No one is really going to help you or give you direction. In fact, the odds are against you."
>
> "You must understand the following: In order to master a field, you must love the subject and feel a profound connection to it. Your interest must transcend the field itself and border on the religious."

ROBERT GREENE
(Best-selling author of Mastery)

DEFINE YOUR NICHE

The next part of defining your podcast is identifying your target market. Without getting into too much marketing jargon, we simply want to create a profile for the person that you are going to be targeting with your podcast episodes. A polarizing thought is this: not everyone will like your podcast. And that's okay. If you're starting a podcast that would interest vegans and vegetarians, then you're never going to get a glowing review and subscription from the bodybuilder that has a steak with every meal (steak and eggs anyone?).

FUN FACT

It is okay to write in this book and fill in answers as you read.
—Marshall Morris

You simply want the specific group of people that would most likely enjoy your podcast and envision them every time you record. Use the following questions to help identify your niche profile:

- Men or Women?

- Interests?

- Age?

- Where do they live?

- Where do they spend their time?

"Conditions are never perfect. 'Someday' is a disease that will take your dreams to the grave with you."

TIM FERRISS
(Best-selling author of The 4-Hour Work Week and one of the top podcasters on the planet. He has invested or advised in startups such as Facebook, Evernote, Shopify, Reputation.com, and TaskRabbit.)

What will also help you in the content section of your podcast is speaking in terms of examples and language that your ideal listener would understand. If your listeners are typically 40-50 years old, then they will not understand the young whippersnapper jargon that all the millennials use. Your goal is to not make the audience feel like they "don't get it" with your jokes, references, and examples. Keep this in your mind.

WHO IS GOING TO BE ON THE PODCAST?

Lastly in defining your podcast, you will need to figure out who will be the hosts of the show. You may find that you only want to plan on yourself as the host of the show (I'm a big fan of this option) because the difficulty of coordinating times to record with another individual can become a gnarly excuse for why the show never got past

Episode #2. Hosting the show yourself can be fun and exciting because you control all of the variables. At times it will be challenging if you've never spoken aloud for 10+ minutes before.

The alternative is to have a co-host that joins you on the show to keep the ball rolling. There are famous duos over the history of broadcasting such as:

- David Letterman and Paul Shaffer on The Late Show

- Kenny "The Jet" Smith and Ernie Johnson on TNT

- Jerry Lewis and Dean Martin from Hollywood

- Penn and Teller from Las Vegas

The trick to finding a good partner for hosting your podcast is someone that is the antithesis (the balanced opposite) of your personality that you can develop chemistry with. On the Thrive Time Show, former US Small Business Administration Entrepreneur of the Year and recovering DJ, Clay Clark, and serial entrepreneur and optometrist Dr. Robert Zoellner complement each other well. Clay serves up business principles real and raw in a way that borders on crossing the line, while Dr. Z serves as a "business yoda" with wisdom that transcends most people's business knowledge. Find a co-host that you can work well with and provide each other with constructive criticism in order to have the most effective partnership.

"Go to ThriveTimeShow.com and listen to "business yoda" Doctor Zoellner and your life will never be the same. He has more talent and mental capacity than I have, yet between the two of us, we have been able to build 13 real multi-million dollar businesses. If we can do it, you can too."

CLAY CLARK
(America's palest male and the owner of numerous chickens, and thousands of trees)

CHAPTER 3

CREATING THE CONTENT

CREATING THE OUTLINE

I'm going to put this bluntly: you MUST create an outline for every podcast. There has never been a successful musician, business owner, performer, or program that hasn't practiced and prepared extensively before performing. This is the hardest part of creating quality content for your podcast. You're going to want to do research, pull quotes, look up statistics, find guests, and rehearse segments before the show recording, or your audience will quickly determine that you have not prepared and will immediately tune you out

"The conventional mind is passive – it consumes information and regurgitates it in familiar forms. The dimensional mind is active, transforming everything it digests into something new and original, creating instead of consuming."

ROBERT GREENE
(The man who continues to be the best-selling author of Mastery)

We went to go see Justin Bieber perform live when he came to town, and I might just be a Belieber now. It was one of the most well-rehearsed performances that I've ever seen from an individual. You can tell that Bieber didn't just start his concert tour by saying "Alright, don't worry about practicing, we're all professionals here. Let's just get out there and hope for the best." My friend, you could tell that he was rehearsing for months in order to get the choreography and music perfect before ever stepping out onto the stage.

You need to approach your podcast episode preparation the same way if you wish to sound professional. Assume the other cohost or guest is not going to be mentally present for your recording and you will need to be able to lead the show recording to the promised land. You and your cohost will always fall to the level of preparation that you require of yourselves.

"When you're around enormously successful people you realize their success isn't an accident – it's about work."

RYAN TEDDER
(Grammy winning recording artist, singer and song-writer who has written hit songs for U2, Adele, OneRepublic, Beyonce, etc...He is become one of the greatest of all time and I went to college with him... Ryan you are an inspiration my man – Clay Clark)

How long should your podcast episodes should be? The ideal is equal to the length of the average commute for your listeners. In most cities, this is going to be 20-30 minutes. You should record for however long you can continue to provide valuable content. Do not rush through your outline without giving your guests any time to respond, nor look for things to filibuster about in order to achieve 30 minutes. For search engine optimization purposes, we suggest recording episodes that are a mimimum of 10 minutes long which creates approximately 1,000 words of content when transcribed.

"Learning to record is like learning to ride a bike. At first you won't be good. Over time you will develop the basic skills and you will want to wave at your mom as you are riding down the street. Then you are going to lose your balance and hit a curb and rip the skin off of your knee. Then your friends are all going to laugh at you and you are going to attempt to play it off like it doesn't hurt, but in reality it's the worst pain you've ever experienced. But then, over time and as a result of practicing, you get better. Strength can only be gained through struggle, so get started failing TODAY so that you can have big success in the near future."

CLAY TIBERIUS CLARK
(A man whose nickname is Claytron because he is known to not take breaks and to not require encouragement or emotional support from anybody)

WHAT DO I SAY? THE FORMAT FOR PODCAST

One of the challenges that I've helped many clients work through is the actual structure for their podcast. It's important to have your show outline printed out onto a piece of paper prior to recording which will allow everyone that is recording to be on the same page as the episode progresses. Don't waste time connecting to the Internet or waiting for your computer to charge in order to pull up the outline digitally – I have NEVER seen this turn out well. Depending on how long your episode is planned to be, your outline will differ slightly from the following template that I have provided you – you may have more content or less.

"Thankfully, persistence is a good substitute for talent."

STEVE MARTIN
(Since the 1980s, having branched away from comedy, Martin has become a successful actor, as well as an author, playwright, pianist, and banjo player, eventually earning an Emmy, Grammy, and American Comedy awards, among other honors. In 2004, Comedy Central ranked Martin at sixth place in a list of the 100 greatest stand-up comics. He was awarded an Honorary Academy Award at the Academy's 5th Annual Governors Awards in 2013.)

1. Pre-roll Advertising

This is the part of the episode that is attached to the beginning of the episode where you can mention sponsors or an exclusive offer for your listeners. This is valuable real estate for your podcast episode as this is the first thing that listeners hear and if it is brief, relevant, and engaging enough, few will skip through it to get to the rest of the episode. This pre-roll advertisement should be about 15 seconds in length.

When you are first getting started, you will not have advertisers or sponsors for this part of the show. Rather, plan on using this short segment to educate your listeners about the nature of your show, why you are doing it, what they will learn, and what it is all about. Think of this as a short elevator pitch.

2. Introduction

One of the most notable things that will set your show apart from hobbyists also making a podcast is a world-class introduction. For example, some of the best introductions I have heard are The Tim Ferriss Podcast (tim.blog/podcast) or the Thrivetime Show (www.ThriveTimeShow.com). The introduction should mention the name of the show, the name of the hosts, a quick rundown of what the show is about, and any catchphrase that you may have. I'd highly recommend getting royalty-free music to mix with your intro from a website like www.audiojungle.net. You do not want to go to jail or pay heavy fines for using music that you do not have licenses to. Do not overthink this step of the process, and there are no rules that say you can't come back and improve the intro later. It will be a brief part of the episode that sets the tone for the rest of the show, so the introduction should be no more than 20-25 seconds.

3. Highlighting Your Main Topic in the first two minutes

This is a huge mistake made by many podcasters from my experience. You must highlight the topic of conversation for that particular episode within the first two minutes of the show. Tell the listener what you are going to be covering in the show, and then tell the audience why it is important that they listen. This does a couple things:

- Your listeners will then know what to look forward to and can determine whether or not they have an interest in this episode, or whether they might want to skip to the next episode.

- For search engine optimization purposes, when the audio is transcribed, the most important topic or keyword will be found at the top of the article and not lost in the middle of the 2nd or third paragraph.

Often times, I think it is easy for hosts to quickly get into a recap for how the weekend went or some other non-related, tangent subject. Make sure that you tell everyone what you plan to talk about on the show first, then you can build the rapport with other hosts and guests.

"There is only one excuse for a speaker's asking the attention of his audience: he must have either truth or entertainment for them."

DALE CARNEGIE
(Best-selling author of The Art of Public Speaking and How to Win Friends and Influence People)

4. Point #1 / "Evergreen" Segment #1

The Topic →

Supporting Statistic →

Supporting Notable Quotation →

A Supporting Story to Illustrate the Concept You are Teaching

This is the main content portion of the podcast. As a host, you will want to tee up the topic and discuss why it is relevant to the listener. These can also be "evergreens" which are segments of the show that are regularly repeated. You'll see these frequently in the most successful shows like The Top 10 on David Letterman's "The Late Show" or SportCenter's Top Plays. Find something that your listeners look forward to every episode. This also immensely helps with your show consistency and preparation.

"You do not deserve to take the audience's time if you have not invested the time needed to prepare."

CARLTON PEARSON
(Best-selling author and former megachurch Pastor of Higher Dimensions Church)

"The will to win is not nearly as important as the will to prepare to win."

VINCE LOMBARDI

(An American football player, coach, and executive in the National Football League [NFL]. He is best known as the head coach of the Green Bay Packers during the 1960s, where he led the team to three straight and five total NFL Championships in seven years, in addition to winning the first two Super Bowls following the 1966 and 1967 NFL seasons.)

There are are several ways to make this interesting for the listeners, but regardless it is important to keep their attention. I suggest using a combination of the following:

1. **A Supporting Statistic**

   Pull a statistic from a credible source that your listeners will recognize. It's important that your statistics aren't pulled from an obscure blog or publication because this will only erode your authority as an expert. No suspicious statistics from BillsRedneckBlog.com about economic development in Minnesota.

2. **A Supporting Quote**

   Same as above. A well-placed quote can be powerful for the listener because it will be something that grabs their attention and is a further supporting thought or idea for your topic from a credible source.

3. **A Supporting Story**

   Stories are powerful. Using them yourself keeps listeners engaged because they want to always know what happens next. Also, asking questions of your guests or cohosts is a skill that the best interviewers have mastered. We talk about the different questions to ask as an interviewer in the next section. Practice telling stories and your content will certainly become more engaging and entertaining.

> "The first problem of communication is getting people's attention."

CHIP HEATH
(Best-selling author of Made to Stick: Why Some Ideas Survive and Others Die)

After you complete one of these content chunks, you will want to transition, or "segue" into the next topic or evergreen. You'll repeat this two or three times as follows:

1. Point #2 / Evergreen Segment #2

   Content → Supporting Statistic → Supporting Quote → Supporting Story

2. Point #3 / Evergreen Segment #3

   Content → Supporting Statistic → Supporting Quote → Supporting Story

3. Mid-roll Advertisement

The next part of the podcast episode will be a break for plugging in a mid-roll, or advertisement placement. Typically this comes about 60% – 75% of the way through the podcast episode. You can use this to plug in an advertiser's pre-recorded ad or talk about a product or service that you use and endorse. Again, I would not include any products or services that you 1) have never used yourself, or 2) endorse with your full faith. Your listeners are precious, you've worked hard to gain a loyal following. The worst thing that you could do is to steer them in the wrong direction for a quick paycheck.

When you first launch your podcast, you may not have any advertisers to fill in here. It is good practice to at least plug something in here, or hook your listeners to your website.

It will help you to sell sponsorships once you are ready for it if you are already in the habit of pausing for an ad or hook.

4. Point #4 / Evergreen Segment #4

Content → Supporting Statistic → Supporting Quote → Supporting Story

5. Point #5 / Evergreen Segment #5

Content → Supporting Statistic → Supporting Quote → Supporting Story

6. Outro

The last part of your podcast episode involves you recapping what was covered during the show.

Many of the most popular podcasts will typically slowly increase the volume of a instrumental song as a signal that the show is wrapping up. More importantly, use the end of the show to give the listener a call to action. What this means is that you must tell them what you want them to do. The following are good ideas for this:

- Go Buy One of Your Specific Products

- Buy Something From the Guest

- Subscribe to Your Podcast

- Download or Request a Free Resource from You

- Visit Your Website

- Email Us Any Questions That You Hvae

"Work to make the core message itself more interesting."

CHIP HEATH
(Best-selling author of Made to Stick: Why Some Ideas Survive and Others Die)

And lastly, you will want to tease the next episode if you have planned for what it will be. Whether it's an exciting guest or a compelling topic, you want to hook the listener with a tease of what is to come in the future.

HOW TO BECOME AN EXCELLENT INTERVIEWER

One of the questions I get asked a lot is how to become a GREAT interviewer. It's true, most of the shows and podcasts that we enjoy feature a phenomenal interviewer. But what makes a great host or interviewer? You simply need to look at the greatest and analyze what they do. My favorites are David Letterman, Oprah Winfrey, Ellen Degeneres, and Jimmy Fallon.

What makes these hosts great? It's simply their ability to create a comfortable environment for their guests to share both real and raw stories as a result of their passion for the subject and their sincere interst in hearing what the guest has to say.

"What you want in an interview is four things: You want someone who can explain what they do very well, who can have a sense of humor and hopefully is self-deprecating, who has a bit of a chip on their shoulder, and passion. If you have passion, a chip on the shoulder, a sense of humor, and you can explain what you do very well, it doesn't matter if you're a plumber or a singer or a politician. If you have those four things, you are interesting."

LARRY KING
(An American television and radio host, whose work has been recognized with awards including two Peabodys and 10 Cable ACE Awards)

Stories allow the guest and host alike to sincerely share an experience that they're not lying about because they are accessing a memory that they do not need to make up, or craft an answer that feels canned and scripted. So as a host, what makes a good story? First, you want to start with the scene of where the story is taking place, and who is involved. What is going on around the situation, and when is the event taking place. Describe what sights, smells, sounds are going on. Help the listener immerse themselves in the situation with you and the guest. Make sure the the story evokes emotion. "When we care, we share." Wharton Business College professor, Jonah Berger, wrote a book titled *Contagious* that talks about why things catch on. I highly recommend it for those looking for additional reading materials about creating viral content that people will want to share. Inside his book *Contagious*, he talks about the 6 ways things will catch on, which you can employ as well.

S – Social Currency – People love being in the know and sharing the link that "everyone just has to see!"

T – Triggers – People love listening to Rebecca Black's song *Friday* becasue it's top of mind. Find a parade and get in front of it!

E – Emotion – People love clicking on images of puppies, babies, and images they connect with.

P – Public – Most people want to do what most other people are doing. Think about the ALS Ice Bucket Challenge.

P – Practical Value – People love to share tips. Think about The Pioneer Woman.

S – Stories – People love to share stories. When you wrap up your business in artisticly cutlivated stories, ideas will spread.

"When we care, we share."

JONAH BERGER
(Best-selling author of Contagious and a professor at the Wharton Business School)

Lastly, add specifics to the story. When the story is vague and ambiguous, it does not feel real. By adding details to the story, your listener will identify their personal experiences that resemble what the guest is talking about.

Too often an interview can feel scripted if all of the questions and answers are rehearsed with the guests. Further, knowing what questions to ask is hugely important. At the same time, the worst thing that you can do is ask a question that paints the guest into a corner or ask something that the guest does not have an intimate knowledge of. I've put together some of my favorite questions I've used and heard asked that consistently invite an interesting response.

1. **Questions To Prompt Your Guest:**

   A. Tell me about the time when you _____...?

   B. Describe the situation when you _____...?

   C. Tell me how you felt when you first _____...?

2. **Questions to Follow-Up:**

   A. Why do you think you felt that way?

   B. How has that been significant in your life?

   C. How did you learn from that experience?

   D. Tell me more about that...?

3. **Questions to Prompt Introspection:**

   A. What would have been the wise thing to do?

   B. If you could give advice to your younger self, what would you say?

   C. It's taken awhile to get to where you are now, what have you learned along your journey that's been the most important? Least important that you should not have spent time on?

   D. In a perfect world, how would this situation look through your eyes?

"Stories carry things. A lesson or moral. Information or a take-home message."

JONAH BERGER
(The man whose name reminds us all of the big whale story, the best-selling author of the book Contagious, and professor at the Wharton Business School)

"The more money you make, the more you will begin to value your time because you will realize that you can make endless amounts of money, but you can't produce more time. Make it your goal to send the smallest e-mail possible when inviting successful people onto your show. Never say anything that is not true and if possible provide a link to something that shows that you actually know what you are talking about. Once I take the time to visit your website, if it is terrible, I'm not going to say "Yes" to the invite. Make sure that your website is well-branded before inviting me to visit your website. We shouldn't judge books by their covers, but we do."

CLAY CLARK
(A man who once cold-called his way into landing the accounts / clients of Boeing, United Airlines, UPS, etc. when running DJConnection.com. The man who once cold-called his way into landing the largest commercial real estate account in Tulsa, Oklahoma with Maurice Kanbar's team Kanbar Properties)

HOW TO INVITE GUESTS ONTO YOUR SHOW

One of the hurdles that I've helped many podcast hosts overcome is how to invite and prepare guests for recording. In order to fully prepare the guest for the show, I recommend sending over an invite and pre-interview questionnaire so that the guest feels as prepared as possible so you can maximize the exposure of the episode once you are ready to publish it. The following is what I would encourage you to customize and send them in an email:

Hey Boss,

I would like to interview you as a featured guest on _____ (name of podcast)

Throughought my career thus far I've been blessed to achieve X, Y, and Z. I would be honored to interview you. Please let me know if I can interview you.

Sincerely,

Clay Clark
Former U.S. Small Business Association Entrepreneur of the Year

"If you give someone a present, and you give it to them in a Tiffany box, it's likely that they'll believe that the gift has higher perceived value than if you gave it to them in no box or a box of less prestige. That's not because the receiver of the gift is a fool. But instead, because we live in a culture in which we gift wrap everything – our politicians, our corporate heads, our movie and TV stars, and even our toilet paper. Public relations (branding) is like gift wrapping."

MICHAEL LEVINE
(The man who has been the public relations consultant of choice for Nike, Pizza Hut, Charlton Heston, Nancy Kerrigan, Michael Jackson, Prince, etc.)

Understand that all of the guests you invite are not going to agree to being on the show. That's okay – not everyone feels comfortable being recorded. Your goal is to help the guests feel the most comfortable possible for the interview. With that being said, understand that the success of the podcast episode cannot be dependent on whether or not your guest has prepared.

You have already blocked off the time and resources to record with your guest, so the last thing that you will want to do is scrap the episode because your guest has not prepared. As a host, you will need to prepare with the mentality that you will need to carry the entire episode and your guest is going to give one word answers. I've seen too many interviews end up as 5 minute episodes because the host had not done sufficient preparation for the episode and had nothing other to say than ask questions. Let the success of your episode be dependent on you (the things you can control) and not others.

"When making sales calls, inviting guests to be on your show or doing anything that might involve you getting rejected you must decide to either be mentally dumb or numb. Really dumb people are usually oblivious to the pain that rejection brings and a healthy dose of novocaine allows a dentist to remove a tooth from your skull without you crying. You are going to get 100 rejections in exchange for every 'yes' you get."

CLAY CLARK
(The man who has built multiple multi-million dollar businesses on the foundation of cold-calling)

CHAPTER 4

BUYING THE EQUIPMENT YOU NEED

Now, we are getting into the nitty gritty specifics of the equipment that you need to record the high quality audio for each podcast. I strongly recommend that you buy the following equipment. However, there are thousands of combinations that could work.

"If you're not a risk taker, you should get the hell out of business."

RAY KROC
(Founder of the McDonald's franchise)

1. The Computer

I recommend buying a computer that was built in the last 3 years so that it is fast enough and updated enough to handle the software you are trying to run. Quit trying to install 2017 versions of Adobe onto your 1999 Micron Computer.

We use Apple computers because they are the most powerful and user friendly. Secondly, you will want to use a computer that has multiple USB (Universal Serial Bus) ports for the microphone and other devices to plug into it.

"Buy the computer you need. Don't make excuses, just buy it. When attending college with Ryan Tedder (Grammy-winning artist) I was always amazed to see this man assembling a music studio item by item in his dorm room. While the other guys on the floor were spending their money on dates, cars, TVs and video games, this man was delaying gratification and concentrating all of the income that he was making waiting tables at Charleston's to buy recording equipment. Stop with the BS about not being able to afford to buy the computer you need and make the tradeoffs you need to get it done."

CLAY CLARK
(A man who worked three jobs simultaneously while living without air-conditioning during a hot Tulsa summer to be able to afford advertising in the Yellow Pages)

2. The Microphone

For basic podcasting, I recommend the Blue Yeti Microphone that you can buy on Amazon.com. It's best for low budget, minimal technology podcasters. It also has a headphone port on the back of it so that you can hear the sweet podcast content you are creating.

For a more professional setup and for advanced podcasters, I'll share the higher quality microphone you would want.

- We use the Electro Voice RE320 ($299)

"As of 2017, if you are serious about podcasting, you should at least believe in yourself enough to buy a RE320 to record your podcast. Also, on a sidenote, if you are going to be shooting womp rats you really need to invest in a quality T-16 Skyhopper."

CLAY CLARK
(The former U.S. SBA Entrepreneur of the Year and a man who loves Star Wars)

- You need an XLR Cable for every microphone you have.

- For these microphones, you will need a Focusrite Scarlett 2i2 Interface for a permanent podcasting location ($149) or a Zoom H6 for mobile podcasting ($349).

- If you are going to have more than 2 people at your permanent podcasting location podcast, get a Focusrite Scarlett 18i8 with 4 microphone inputs.

"Buy the Electro Voice RE320 ($299) and quit saying you can't afford it. Turn off your TV, quit gambling, stop smoking, stop drinking, or get another job... just get it done."

CLAY CLARK
(The man who was named Tulsa's Entrepreneur of the Year by the Chamber of Commerce at the age of 20 as a result of being able to live below his means and to go without TV, air-conditioning, and other thing that many people would not be able to go without)

3. The Headphones

For podcasters, it's important that you monitor the audio levels that are recording. I've seen many interviews that are not usable because the guest or host drifted too far away from the microphone, and rendered it unusable. If you are using headphones, then you will be able to correct immediately if there is a problem rather than find out an hour into recording. Encourage everyone on the show to stay as close to the microphone as possible. As far as which specifically to get, I prefer the following:

- Shure SRH440 Studio Headphones – $99

- AKG K142 Headphones – $89

"Don't spend $600 on your headphones. Get the headphones Marshall has recommended. Spend your war-chest on promoting, marketing and advertising your podcast."

CLAY CLARK
(The former U.S. Small Business Administration Entrepreneur of the Year)

4. Software

Just like the hardware, there's all kinds of programs you COULD use, but don't debate me, and just use the following options.

Podcasting Software

Adobe Audition – Download at Adobe.com

You can sign up for a software subscription plan and they make it very easy to use. In the next section we show you how to use it.

Call Recording Software (for guest interviews not in the same location)

Skype – Computer-to-Computer Calling - Download at Skype.com

With Skype, you can make free computer-to-computer calls and affordable long distance calls which is the best solution for connecting with your guests for interviews.

Movavi – Skype & Screen Recorder - Download at movavi.com

After starting a call with Skype, you will need to record the audio from the call. Movavi allows you to record the audio and video from a Skype call and offers an extensive list of walkthroughs for how to use the system.

CHAPTER 5

RECORDING YOUR PODCAST

"We don't like checklists. They can be painstaking. They're not much fun. But I don't think the issue here is mere laziness. There's something deeper, more visceral going on when people walk away not only from saving lives but from making money. It somehow feels beneath us to use a checklist, an embarrassment. It runs counter to deeply held beliefs about how the truly great among us—those we aspire to be—handle situations of high stakes and complexity. The truly great are daring. They improvise. They do not have protocols and checklists. Maybe our idea of heroism needs updating."

ATUL GAWANDE
(Harvard Medical School professor and best-selling author of The Checklist Manifesto: How to Get Things Right)

In order to make your life at least 2% easier. I've provided a detailed walkthrough of setting up your podcasting software (specifically Adobe Audition). Your ability to stay organized and do the same thing every time is what will allow your podcast to be sustainable. If you do not use a checklist or workflow, then you will miss steps and forget to do things.

The following is a checklist to get you started recording in Adobe Audition TODAY. I've set this up on a Mac computer, so a PC will appear slightly different. If you have any questions, please email us at Info@Thrive15.com.

HOW TO RECORD A PODCAST

1. Open Adobe Audition

2. Go to File > New > Multitrack Session...

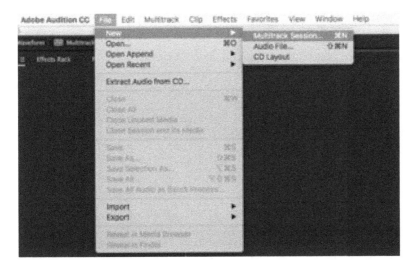

3. Name the Session with the DATE and Podcast Company Name as shown below, then click "Browse..." Ex. "6.28.17 – Thrive15"

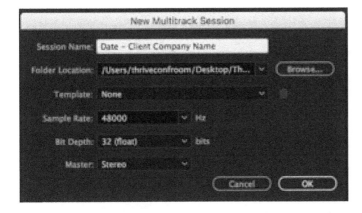

Book Your Tickets to the next in-person 2–day ThriveTimeShow. com workshop and you can actually schedule a time to watch a recording of the 2–hour ThriveTime Business Coach Radio Show

4. Click Documents on the left hand side. If it's your first time podcasting on this computer, create a folder by clicking New Folder button in the bottom left corner of the window. Name it the podcast name. If you have previously podcasted on this computer, select the podcast's folder in Documents.

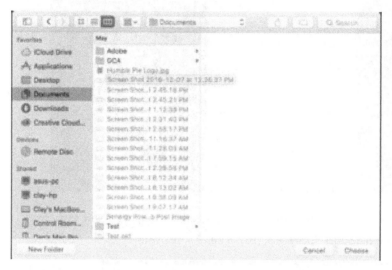

5. Set the setting as indicated in the screenshot below and click OK.

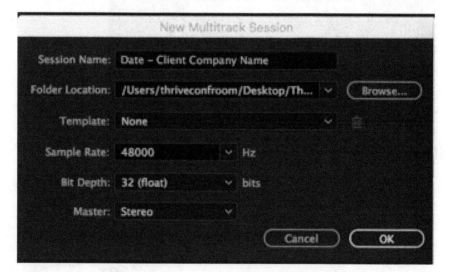

6. Click Adobe Audition CC in Top Navigation Bar > Preferences… and Click Audio Hardware.

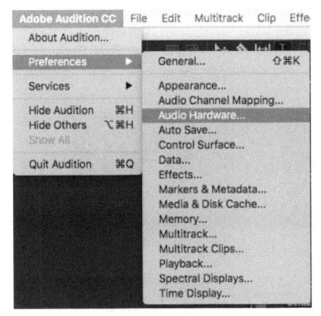

7. Verify that your microphone (or Scarlett 2i2 USB) is selected for Default Input and Default Output, and then click OK.

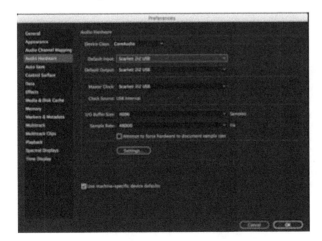

8. For the Blue Yeti Microphone setups: On Track 1, make sure the right arrow is set to Mono > Blue Yeti Microphone.

9. For multiple microphones setups with the Scarlett:
On Track 1, make sure the right arrow is set to Mono > [01M] Scarlett 2i2 USB: Input 1. On Track 2, make sure the right arrow is set to Mono > [02M] Scarlett 2i2 USB: Input 2.

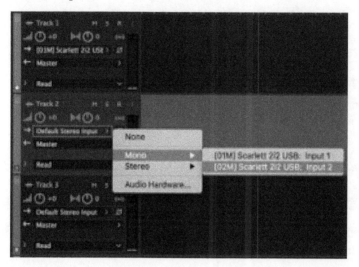

10. Click the R so it turns red for Track 1, and click the R so it turns red for Track 2 (if there are multiple microphones).

11. Press Red Circle at Bottom of Window to Start Recording an episode:

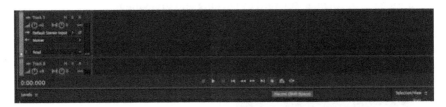

12. Record for 10 minutes:

    A. State which Podcast Episode # it is and Podcast/Company Name

    B. State the topic within the first two sentences

    C. Introduce Yourself and Company

    D. Mention your SEO keyword at least 6 times throughout the podcast episode.

13. Once the 10 minutes is complete, click the square icon at the bottom of the window.

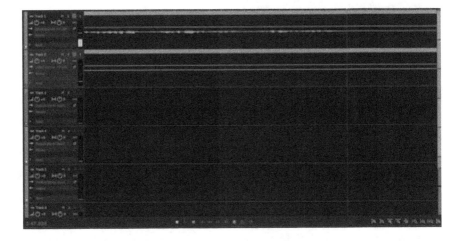

14. Once stopped, if you are going to record another episode, move the cursor (blue upside down triangle) forward by clicking and dragging it.

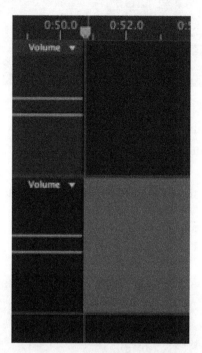

15. To export the episode, start by Zooming Out so you can see an entire episode. You can do this by pressing the minus key on the keyboard (to the right of the 0).

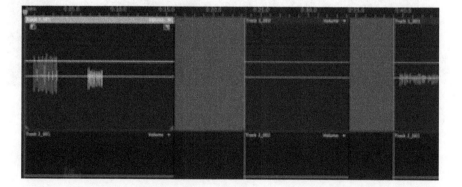

16. Drag the Blue Playhead (upside down triangle) by clicking and dragging to the beginning of where an episode starts.

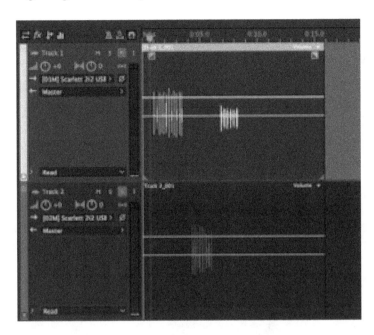

17. Press the letter i:

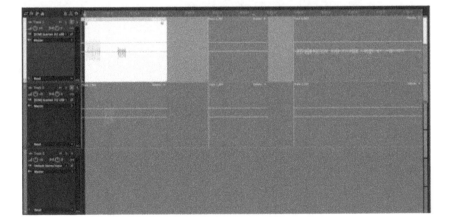

18. Drag the Blue Playhead (upside down triangle) by clicking and dragging to the beginning of where an episode ends.

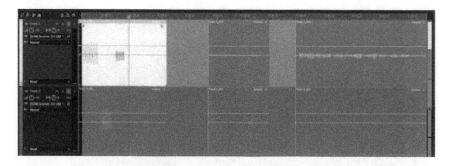

19. Press the letter o:

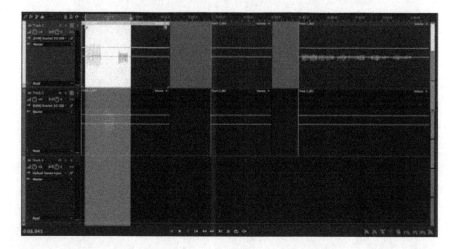

20. With the episode highlighted, select File > Export... > Multitrack Mixdown > Time Selection...

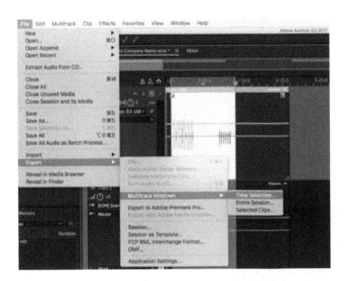

21. Click Browse...

22. Name the File under Save As... as follows:

    A. Podcast Number - Podcast Name

    B. Example: 16 - ThrivetimeShow

23. Click Documents

24. Click Your Podcast Exports Folder

25. Click Save

26. Make sure the settings are the same as below

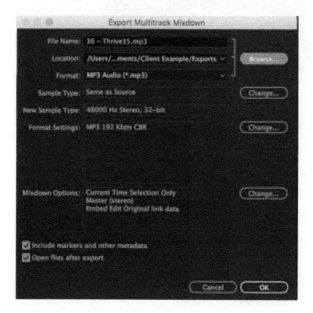

27. Click OK

"Always deliver more than expected."

LARRY PAGE
(Co-founder of Google)

CHAPTER 6

HOSTING YOUR PODCAST

Once you have recorded and exported your podcast episode, you will need to decide where your listeners will actually want to listen to your podcast. Ultimately there are two options for hosting your podcast.

"Do not get stuck or overwhelmed. If you can't figure it out that does not mean you are mildly retarded it just means that you need attend an in person ThriveTimeShow. com 2-Day Workshop so that our team can show you in-person how to setup your podcast. It's not your fault if you struggle to understand a new concept. However, it is your fault if you decide to allow yourself to stay stuck."

CLAY CLARK
(The founder of ThriveTimeShow.com)

YOUR OWN WEBSITE

If you want more control of creating a brand around your podcast, you will want to host your podcast on your own website. There are three things that you need:

Wordpress Website – Free –wordpress.org

As part of our coaching program, for less money than it would cost you to hire one full-time $8.25 per hour employee, we will build a search engine friendly and podcast listener friendly website.

Smart Podcast Player Plugin – $8/mo –smartpodcastplayer.com

This is the player that will be used on your site. It's a plugin (or something you install on Wordpress) that you will activate on your website. It's a user-friendly system that some of the biggest podcasters use.

It's the same system that John Lee Dumas has used EOFire.com. It's the same system that Michael Hyatt uses with THIS IS YOUR LIFE™ PODCAST. Just use this.

BluBrry Powerpress Plugin – Free – www.blubrry.com

This is the part of the system that creates an RSS feed which you will need to submit to iTunes. RSS stands for "Really Simple Syndication" or "Rich Site Summary", a family of web feed formats.

BONUS: BluBrry Podcast Statistics – $5/month – www.blubrry.com

If you are very interested in the number of downloads, where they are coming from, and number of subscribers (you need this if you plan to monetize the podcast itself), then you will need a way to track your numbers. This is what the Thrivetime Show has used for our podcast.

For added convenience, I have created a video training that explains the process of hosting your own show and shows a tutorial that you can use while following along with your own website. Simply email me at Info@Thrive15.com.

"You shouldn't focus on why you can't do something, which is what most people do. You should focus on why perhaps you can, and be one of the exceptions."

STEVE CASE
(Co-founder of AOL)

DIRECT HOSTING

For those looking for an easy, out-of-the-box podcast hosting solution, I would recommend using Soundcloud.com. Soundcloud.com is a platform used by musicians, artists, and podcasters alike to showcase their audio creations. The basic membership is free, while as you grow, you will likely need to upgrade to a paid membership account. Just like if you were to host your podcast on your own website, you still need to create an RSS feed. Again, this is what other platforms (ie. iTunes) will use to automatically update their stores and platforms whenever you post a new episode. You can access this from inside the settings of your account under Content.

Settings

Account Content **Notifications** **Privacy**

RSS feed ⑦

RSS feed
http://feeds.soundcloud.com/users/soundcloud:users:1110362/sounds.rss

Email address displayed

Custom feed title

Category *

Stats–service URL prefix ⑦
http://

Custom author name

Language *
English

Subscriber redirect ⑦
http://

☐ Contains explicit content

Upload Defaults ⑦

☑ Include in RSS feed
☐ Creative Commons license

Cancel   Save changes

Using this system is a simple way to get your podcast to your audience. The reason why most advanced podcasters don't like it is because you are limited with the branding (logo, colors, etc.) that you can do on your Soundcloud.com account. If you are okay with making that tradeoff, it is perfect for beginners.

If you feel stuck, book a ticket for our next workshop and we will give you a personal walk-through of how this entire process works. Book your tickets today at ThriveTimeShow.com.

"A person who never made a mistake never tried anything new."

ALBERT EINSTEIN
(A legendary physicist who pushed President Roosevelt to allow him to create the atom bomb before the German's completed their atomic weapon. Without Albert Einstein, America would have lost World War II)

CHAPTER 7

STRATEGIZING FOR LAUNCH

By now, you've gone through the grueling tasks of getting all of the things you need to launch the podcast, spent more time than you thought getting the hang of the recording and finding your podcast personality, and you've learned to navigate the technology for hosting your podcast. Now it's time to put it out there for the world to see. It's important to understand the following concept: nobody is going to wake up with a burning desire to pay you, and nobody is going to wake up with a burning desire to listen to your podcast. "That didn't seem very motivational, Marshall…" I know. Which is why this chapter is so important to leverage the novelty of a new podcast and how to acquire new subscribers.

"Risk more than others think is safe. Dream more than others think is practical."

HOWARD SCHULTZ
(CEO of Starbucks)

In 2013, Apple iTunes passed the 1 billion podcast subscriptions threshold (macworld.com). That is a massive number of people that have chosen to get their content and information from the podcast format. In fact, that number comes from over 250,000 different unique podcasts and over 8 million episodes. The iTunes Store is one of the best places to find your new podcast listeners online and begin growing your audience and subscriptions. We will teach you how to launch on iTunes in the next chapter, and the strategy behind it in this one.

The process is simple. In order to capitalize on the new release of your podcast on iTunes, you want to become a podcast featured in one of the coveted spots on the New & Noteworthy section on iTunes. As in anything, you must create a quality product in order for it to get talked about.

"I'm convinced that about half of what separates the successful entrepreneurs from the non-successful ones is pure perseverance."

STEVE JOBS
(Co-founder and CEO of Apple)

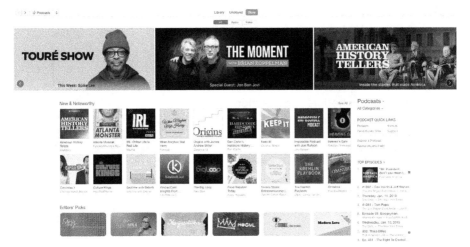

"In a crowded marketplace, fitting in is failing. In a busy marketplace, not standing out is the same as being invisible. Remarkable products and people get talked about. Boring is invisible."

SETH GODIN
(Bestselling author of Purple Cow. He used $20,000 in savings to found Seth Godin Productions, primarily a book packaging business, out of a studio apartment in New York City. He then met Mark Hurst and founded Yoyodyne. In 1998, he sold Yoyodyne to Yahoo! for about $30 million and became Yahoo's vice president of direct marketing)

"You try to do the best with what you've got and ignore everything else. That's why horses get blinders in horse racing: You look at the horse next to you, and you lose a step."

JIMMY IOVINE
(Legendary record producer who has sold over 250 million albums and the genius mastermind both Interscope Records and Beats Headphones)

"You must take the time to schedule all of your action items into your calendar. You must actually do this or you will just become overwhelmed with ideas and you won't start. Schedule these action items into your calendar now."

CLAY CLARK
(Former U.S. Small Business Administration Entrepreneur of the Year)

If there is a buzz around your show from the beginning, iTunes will recognize that and want to promote your show in order to feature quality content to its users. This is hugely important because one you are promoted to the New & Noteworthy section, your growth can snowball as you acquire more listeners and subscribers.

So how do you become featured in the New & Noteworthy section of iTunes. You need to become one of the top 100 hottest and fastest growing podcasts released in the last 8 weeks. That's right. You only have 8 weeks to be featured in the New & Noteworthy section, so it's important that you make sure that you've put yourself in the best position to be recognized and featured. Here are the following things to make sure you do:

Create Quality Episodes
Nobody is going to stick around to listen if you are not engaging.

Hook Your Subscribers

In each episode, you are going to want to ask your listeners to do two things:

1) Go to iTunes to subscribe

2) Go listen to a previous episode, or get them excited for the next one

Maintain a High Download Count

It's best if you already have people that have downloaded and listened to your podcast creating a high download count from the beginning before you submit it to iTunes. You can achieve this by sending your episodes to family & friends, sharing on social media, and distributing where to listen.

Release With Multiple Episodes

I recommend getting at least 5 episodes completed and posted before releasing, and 5 more (10 total) ready to be posted regularly after you launch on iTunes. This gives your new listeners an opportunity to listen to more episodes after they fall in love with you (and I know they will), and more likely to become a subscriber. It's also a great way to drive more downloads. If you have 5 episodes already posted and you get 10 new subscribers, that can amount to 50 new downloads! However, if you start with only 1 or 2 episodes, and have 10 new subscribers, that would result in only 10-20 downloads.

Follow All of iTunes Rules

If you are not submitting a quality photo, a complete description, good episode titles and description, then iTunes is likely to keep you from the New & Noteworthy section because they do not want to promote a poor-looking album image.

Get Reviews

Once you submit to iTunes, it will be important to manually solicit reviews from your listeners on your podcast episode.

Further, make sure that your friends and family members that like your podcast are reviewing you. The more engagement that your podcast has on iTunes, the more likely your podcast will be featured on the New & Noteworthy section.

"Do not be embarrassed by your failures, learn from them and start again."

RICHARD BRANSON
(th dyslexic founder of Virgin Group who started his first business, a newspaper, after dropping out of high school and in spite of his struggle to actually read)

With all of these factors contributing to your overall ranking on iTunes, the last point for all of these things is consistency. Google will not promote your business to the top of search results if you are spamming them, and iTunes will not promote you if you are caught spamming them either. If you get a bunch of reviews immediately, but then never ask or receive another ever again, then you will be less likely to retain high ranking. Make an effort to go out and solicit real reviews from real listeners consistently and your efforts will pay off.

CHAPTER 8

SUBMITTING YOUR PODCAST TO ITUNES

It's time: time to launch on iTunes. There are not a lot of things that need to be said about this, so here is the simple checklist for how to get your podcast onto iTunes.

"Half the battle is selling music, not singing it. It's the image, not what you sing."

ROD STEWART
(Born and raised in London, he is of Scottish and English ancestry. Stewart is one of the best-selling music artists of all time, having sold over 100 million records worldwide. He has had six consecutive number one albums in the UK and his tally of 62 UK hit singles includes 31 that reached the top ten, six of which gained the #1 position. Stewart has had 16 top ten singles in the US, with four reaching #1 on the Billboard Hot 100)

Create an Apple ID

The first thing you will need to distribute your podcast on iTunes is to create an Apple ID if you do not have one. Most people will already have a personal Apple ID from using iTunes, the App Store, or buying an Apple Product.

Log into Podcasts Connect

You will use your Apple ID to log into the platform that manages the podcast you want to submit to iTunes. Log in at podcastsconnect.apple.com.

Verify Your RSS Feed is Setup

In order to distribute the right information about your podcast and its episodes, you need to setup the RSS feed information in PowerPress (your website), or Soundcloud.com (your direct hosting).

- iTunes Program Title

- iTunes Album Image (2000px by 2000px)

- iTunes Program Subtitle

- iTunes Program Summary

- Your summary cannot exceed 4,000 characters in length and should not include HTML, except for hyperlinks

- iTunes Category

- iTunes Explicit - yes/no

- iTunes Author Name

- iTunes Email

If you would like the video training for either of these, in my shameless attempt to make your life 2% easier, simply email us at info@Thrive15.com.

Submit your Podcast RSS Feed - Once the feed information has been filled out, you can submit your podcast to iTunes at podcastsconnect.apple.com. Once it is submitted, it will take a day or two to get approved and launched into the iTunes Store.

CHAPTER 9

GROWING AN AUDIENCE

Holy crap. Your podcast is live…..now what? You have successfully accomplished what most of your friends and family have always told you that THEY were going to do someday, but never actually did. You stared back into the face of adversity & procrastination and actually LAUNCHED a podcast. Now comes the fun part. Building your audience.

"Marketing is a contest for people's attention."

SETH GODIN
(Author of numerous New York Times best-selling books)

There's many different automations, funnels, and methods that other books or people will tell you to set up. If you look at the most successful marketers for any product or podcast, they all share a common underlying similarity: the rate of engagement of their audiences. No click funnel can replace actually reaching out and connecting with an individual that listens or appears on your podcast. So when we talk about the following ways to create engagement and build your audience, I DO want to scale it in a sustainable way.

I DO NOT want you to take out the human element of connection that may save you time (which in reality will require more time because your friend pushing a hot new Customer Relationship Management Program (CRM) that sends endless drip marketing emails that not even yourself reads is a substantial amount of time to learn and then realize that the return on your investment but more importantly your time is not worth it).

Post When a New Episode is Live

The first thing that you need to do when you release a new podcast episode is to post on your social media and platforms that a new episode is live. When you post about it, make sure to include an image; on social media, people are drawn to visually stimulating posts. Also, include the guest and/or topic that you are featuring with a brief description to hook somebody looking at the post. This is NOT "click bait" irrelevant to the main focus of your episode.

This IS the most important part of your episode that is attractive enough that will get a listener to download your episode.

click·bait klikbāt

> **Noun**
>
> Origin language: Jackassery

Definition: (on the Internet) deceiving content whose main purpose is to attract attention and encourage visitors to click on a link to a particular web page. "These recent reports of the show's imminent demise are hyperbolic clickbait"

"If your podcast is terrible focus on making it not terrible. Then focus on making it good. Then focus on making it great. Then focus on marketing it. Do not go out there and spend thousands of dollars marketing something that is terrible."

CLAY CLARK
(The man who built the award-winning DJConnection.com entertainment company)

When you post make sure that you commit to posting to whichever social media platforms you have chosen to be part of your official brand.

I recommend Twitter + one other platform. Again, consistency in creating a valuable social media account where you post every time an episode is live and in a timely fashion is critical.

Furthermore, not only should you be leveraging followers on your podcast's social media accounts, but also your own personal accounts. Some of the clients that I have worked with have felt shameful not wanting to push their episode to their friends on social media for fear of them being "defriended." Hilarious. To that I would say that you can expect zero downloads and subscriptions. I would not recommend spamming your contacts with invaluable content. However, when you start your business, brand, or podcast, you ARE the brand. Utilize the tools and the network of people that you have at your disposal to make your audience great.

Email When a New Episode is Live

The next thing that you can do to leverage your audience and following of your podcast is to email a subscriber list. You will need to begin building a list of interested followers, and typically this takes form as a popup on a website, or a form that a listener fills out. Many successful podcasters have created an email list that is interested in knowing when the next episode is live so that they can be sure to listen to it. You can ask people to opt-in to an email list that notifies them when a new episode is live. This is a way to quickly grow an audience and ensure that they are getting the newest content that is released (and increasing your downloads).

Email Guest When a New Episode is Live

One of the most valuable things that you can do when you release a new episode is that you can engage any guest that is on the episode. You will find that these individuals are some of your biggest advocates and best marketers. This is for a few reasons:

People's Favorite Topic is Themselves

In a shameless attempt to promote themselves, your guests will share the episode to their audience and followers. This further provides valuable content to them and validates your guest as an expert among their own followers.

Your Guest's Network

By asking your guest to promote the podcast episode to his or her audience, you are going to reach an entirely new group of people that hear your podcast. If you simply ask the same group of people through traditional marketing methods, you may exhaust your ability to acquire any new subscribers to your podcast. With the power of a referral from a guest, you will arrive in front of many new ears hearing your podcast for the first time. Additionally, there is a chance that your guest's audience is already much larger than yours. So even if their audience is composed of people that would also appreciate your brand, this can stimulate your growth by getting you in front of more people faster.

"Don't email your guests in a SPAM like, click-funnel BS kind of way. Treat your guests like someone that you are dating and actively trying to woo. Be thoughtful and intentional."

CLAY CLARK
(The former U.S. Small Business Administration Entrepreneur of the Year who started his first business in his parent's basement and then he scaled it out of his college dorm room)

So when you reach out to a guest to let them know that his or her podcast is live, this is what you need to remember and include: Email them early in the morning of the day that the episode is live. Text them early in the morning of the day that the episode is live. Facebook them in the morning of the day that the episode is live. Thank them for appearing on the podcast. Include the link to where the episode is hosted.

Provide a short description of the episode that they can share to their audience .

Ask them to share it to their audience.

Ask for a 5-Star Review on iTunes.

Engaging on Social Media

Lastly, you will want to engage with your audience on social media. Between episodes, you will have listeners that want to connect with you further. Provide them a social media platform where they can ask questions, connect with other listeners, and get additional content. Whether this is your website (like ThrivetimeShow.com), or another social media platform, make sure that whichever you direct them to is being monitored. The whole point of engagement is that YOU engage.

Too frequently I will see podcast hosts drive traffic to a social media platform and then automate a response or hire a virtual assistant to answer everything. I think you should leverage your time and be proactive in your responses; however, if you do not participate in the conversations going on about your podcast episodes, then you will never develop a meaningful connection. Those meaningful connections are what help you virally grow and, eventually, get you paid.

"The media wants overnight successes (so they have someone to tear down). Ignore them. Ignore the early adopter critics who never have enough to play with. Ignore your investors who want proven tactics and predictable instant results. Listen instead to your real customers, to your vision, and make something for the long haul. Because that's how long it's going to take."

SETH GODIN
(The man who continues to be the legendary marketing expert and best-selling author of numerous books)

With that being said, DO NOT spend endless amounts of time on social media. Your business or podcast is what should occupy your time, not responding to social media posts and browsing insights. Proactively schedule the time every day that you will respond to messages, answer questions, and post content in between episodes. This process should not consume the majority of your time. In fact, you should do all of your critical thinking at one time and schedule your posts using Hootsuite.com. I unfortunately do not make any money from referring them, but I will advocate for them because of the time freedom they provide me.

As part of the ThrivetimeShow.com we knew that we needed daily content for our platform on social media in addition to the daily radio shows we broadcast. Rather than spending the one hour per day to address this to make sure a social media marketer was spelling everything correctly and following brand guidelines, the leadership team locked ourselves away for a week and a half to write, edit, and approve every post for THE NEXT TWO YEARS.

It was a grind. It was not fun. But it was finished. With Hootsuite.com, we were able to schedule the posts that links to all of our social media platforms and not think about what we were positing for the day ever again. In addition, we can still post timely and relevant content as it comes up, but now we don't need to worry about not posting for a day.

"Consistency is super important with any type of marketing. We designed our social media posts to be consistent and relevant to our niche focus of ideal and likely buyers (entrepreneurs) and then when something unpredictable and relevant happens we will make a social media post about it (The NFL's Patriots winning a game, one of our business coach clients experiencing a big win, opening up another Elephant In The Room Men's Grooming Lounge location (EITRLounge. com) or OXIFresh.com celebrating the 100,000th Google Review)."

CLAY CLARK
(The former U.S. Small Business Administration Entrepreneur of the Year)

"The way to get started is to quit talking and begin doing."

WALT DISNEY
(The man who started the Disney empire after famously losing it all twice. Imagine how he must have felt, but he did not quit)

CHAPTER 10

MAKING MONEY FROM PODCASTING

I was helping a client a couple years ago, and she was really having a hard time understanding what she needed to do to turn her passion into a job. She is a holistic health coach in her mid-twenties that sincerely wanted to help people by providing them information on what they can do to optimize their life. She wanted to do this full-time, but was struggling to see the path for how this could replace her income. We went through what her goals were and identified that podcasting might be an appropriate vehicle to help get her content in front of people. She lit up with enthusiasm. She LOVED podcasts, she listened to them everyday. However, starting a podcast does NOT mean that you can immediately start making money from it. For her, it was important that she created some kind of income while she grew her podcast audience size.

Podcasting is not a "get rich quick" scheme (in fact, there is no such thing - we can debate another time). However, you CAN make money from it. This is the gap that many podcasters never bridge either because they are not able to grow the podcast to where it needs to be or they do not know what to do in order to leverage the success of their content. If you are not passionately interested in generating revenue from your podcast, or maybe you are creating a podcast as merely a hobby or for SEO, you can skip this chapter. For everyone else, let's begin.

Sponsorships

One of the most popular and traditional ways of earning money from your podcast is sponsorship revenue. This is where a company will approach a podcast owner and negotiate a sum of money for their company's brand sponsorship to the listeners of the podcast.

This is both a scary and exciting time for your podcast because what this means is that you have provided enough valuable content that another company has recognized that you are in front the ideal and likely buyers they want to be in front of. It also means that you are going to be promoting somebody other than yourself alongside you and potentially diluting your content.

When you first start your podcast, you are going to have zero downloads, zero subscribers, and zero content. Unless you have a loyal following like Michael Bolton (just kidding) before you launch, you will not be able to attract any advertisers on

This man (Michael Bolton) has sincerely sold over 75 million records.

your show. As you grow your audience, and your brand begins to build, more and more buzz will be created around the show. You will attract a very specific niche of people that are interested in the same things that you are. As that niche of people begins to build and refine, advertisers will take notice and at that tipping point, they will reach out to begin a sponsorship or partnership. Let me give you an example.

When we first started the Thrivetime Show, we knew that we were not going to have any subscribers. That's why we understood that no matter how hard we tried, it would be difficult to sell ads to companies looking to reach a small number of subscribers. In fact, we committed to recording daily even prior to partnering with Scripps Media. Why is this? "You mean you guys recorded daily without any type of promise or agreement that you would get paid?" Absolutely. When we first started discussing the thoughts of broadcasting a daily show on both podcast and the radio, experienced radio executives were skeptical. And they should be.

Most people cannot do anything daily without any loss of interest and commitment. So we committed ourselves to proving that we would release a daily show rain or shine, health or sickness, inclement weather or sunny skies. What the radio station executives wanted was consistency, which few people are able to provide. And that is exactly what your advertisers will want if they are going to spend copious amounts of money ahead of time in order to be featured on your episodes. With the Thrivetime Show, we found that after about 100 episodes of diligently recording, uploading, broadcasting, and marketing our episodes, we were able to become an official show for Scripps Media (the same guys that own the Travel Channel, Food Network, and many more) and begin signing sponsorship deals.

The core of a sponsorship deal is that it is a win-win for the parties involved. The sponsors that approached us were those that wanted to connect and be in front of the listeners that we attracted. But what exactly do you sell them? Great question, and let's get into it.

There are two main "products" you can sell as a sponsorship for a podcast, and those are a 1) Pre-Roll advertisement, and a 2) Mid-Roll advertisement. Typically these are sold together for one episode at a time.

 Pre-Roll

As discussed in the content section of this book, the Pre-Roll advertisement appears at the beginning of the episode, and typically lasts about 15 seconds. You have flexibility as the podcast host, but most podcasters and advertisers will agree that the best place for the Pre-Roll is immediately following the introduction.

 Mid-Roll

The other part of advertisements on podcast episodes are the mid-roll commercials. These typically will appear 60%-75% of the way through the episode. This is actually very useful if you are going to have to edit any parts of your interview (I suggest not to if possible ie. Time Ferriss never goes back and edits his podcast) because you have recorded the interview separate from the rest of the podcast episode. These commercials are usually 45-60 seconds in length - long enough to provide additional information about a product or service and give important details of the call to action.

 How Much Money Can I Make?

Understand that as the podcast host, it is entirely up to you how much you ultimately will sell a sponsorship package for. With that being said, there are standards for approximately where to begin your pricing strategy. For example, a 15-second pre-roll advertisement is close to $20 per 1,000 people that listen to it. For a longer, 60-second Mid-Roll advertisement, you can charge $25 per 1,000 people that listen.

If you have 5,000 people that are subscribed to your show, then the numbers add up quickly.

$20 + $25 = $45 * 5

$45 * 5 (for 5,000 subscribers) = $225

$225 * # of episodes per month = Monthly Sponsorship Revenue

      Bi-Weekly = $225 * 2 = $450 per month

      Weekly = $225 * 4 = $900 per month

      Daily = $225 * 30 = $6,750 per month

You can easily see how the sponsorship monetization of your podcast can quickly scale with the consistency of how many shows you regularly produce.

So who are you going to ask to advertise on you show? Furthermore, what are you going to say? Start by really identifying who your ideal and likely listener is. Then, make a list of all of the other companies that also share this same set of demographics as you. The next part is the scary part: reach out to them! All you need to do is begin by crafting an email that includes the following:

- Tell them who you are and what the podcast is

- Give a brief description of the podcast and a link to a recent, relevant episode

- Give a description of who the audience is

- Mention any stats or metrics that contribute to the success of your podcast

- Specify why advertising on your podcast would benefit their company

- Use an email, followed, by a handwritten note, followed by a phone call to gauge their interest in whether or not they would be a good fit as an advertising sponsor. This process can be tough and scary, but fear not. You are a brave podcaster.

In fact, Scripps Media (the owner of our show) has recognized the value of this process so for podcast hosts that do not want to negotiate with advertisers themselves, they actually partnered with a company called MidRoll.com that will do all of that for you and your podcast if you meet certain criteria. This is a great way to begin earning money on your podcast without having to go through the process of identifying interested companies that would be a good fit for your podcast.

Affiliate Links

The next way to monetize your podcast and turn it into a full-time job (should you choose) is to host an affiliate link. Most national companies that sell a product or a service will offer some type of affiliate program where they will provide you a unique link or code that credits a sale on their website to you, and in turn, gives you a commission from that sale. This can be a powerful way to earn money. NOTE: I would caution you against recommending anything that you have not used yourself or are not 100% confident in. Your audience is a precious group of people that you have worked hard to build. You don't want to send them to something that will not truly benefit them for the sake of earning an affiliate commission.

> "If you can't sell, your business will go to hell. Dial and smile and call them all until they cry, buy, or die!"

CLAY CLARK
(Host of the ThriveTime Business Coach Radio Show)

 ## Selling a Product

The third way I would recommend monetizing your podcast would be to drive listeners to a website or place where they can purchase one of your products or services. If you are going to turn your podcast into a business or marketing pipeline, then you must drive sales. You are going to commit a large amount of time to making the podcast great, so make sure that you capitalize on your hard work by providing a call to action for your listeners. You do not need, millions upon millions of listeners in order to become incredibly wealthy. What you need is 1,000 "true fans."

"Simply put, you need 1,000 people that are extremely happy with what you provide, not millions. In fact, trying to satisfy millions is exhausting. These listeners download all of the episodes. These listeners engage on social media. These listeners take advantage of the resources that you provide and recommend. If you have only 1,000 true fans around the country, it is as easy as developing a $100 product or service that they will be interested in.

Selling a $100 product or service to 1,000 people is far easier than selling a $1 product to 1 million people."

KEVIN KELLY
(Co-founder of Wired Magazine)

CHAPTER 11

CONCLUSION

YOU'VE DONE IT.

You are on your way to becoming a worldclass podcaster. I sincerely believe that you can apply these steps in your own podcast to achieve the success that you are wanting. Success is not created by luck. There is no such thing as "get rich quick." You are the master of your own fate. Podcasting is a world that I have gotten very excited about in the past 5 years because of both the time and financial freedom it can provide. For your valuable content and coaching, you are no longer shackled to the mere 1-to-1 ratio of people that you can help. Now, you can scale your vision and provide practical training to millions across the world. If you have any questions about this book or would like to connect, please email us at Info@Thrive15.com. This is your year to THRIVE. I'm excited for your success.

Marshall Morris

"Rise and Grind! It's profound everyday you are above the ground. This BOOM is for you. **BOOM!**"

CLAY CLARK
(Former U.S. Small Business Administration Entrepreneur of the Year)

ACTION ITEMS

1. Pass on what you've learned by writing a Google Review. Type in "Thrive15 Jenks" and write that review today!

2. Don't miss a radio show or podcast. Subscribe and review us on iTunes at ThriveTimeShow.com.

3. Get all of the interactive downloadables by signing up today at ThriveTimeShow.com.

WANT MORE?

Check out the Ultimate Textbook for Starting, Running & Growing Your Own Business!

Start Here

NEVER before has entrepreneurship been delivered in an UNFILTERED, real and raw way... until now. This book is NOT for people that want a politically correct and silver-lined happy-go-lucky view of entrepreneurship. That's crap. Supported by case studies and testimonials from entrepreneurs that have grown their businesses all over the planet using these best practice systems, former U.S. Small Business Administration Entrepreneur of the Year, Clay Clark, shares the specific action steps for successful business systems, hilarious stories from situations that every entrepreneur faces, and entrepreneurship factoids that are guaranteed to blow your mind.

Invite a Friend to Join You at the World's Best 2-Day Intensive Business Workshop

Get specific and practical training on how to grow your business

Book your tickets today at ThriveTimeShow.com

CPSIA information can be obtained
at www.ICGtesting.com
Printed in the USA
LVHW031041060120
642629LV00006B/777/P